Here's to Strong Women

Women

Anthology II

Stephanie Ford

Get Cha Mind Right, Inc.

PHILADELPHIA, PA

ISBN-10: 9780578505664
Library of Congress Cataloging-in-Publication Date is available.

Project Specialist, Barlow Enterprises, LLC

Legal Disclaimer

While none of the stories in this book are fabricated, some of the names and details may have been changed to protect the privacy of the individuals mentioned. Although the author and publisher have made every effort to ensure that the information in this book was correct at press time, the author and publisher do not assume and hereby disclaim any liability to any party for any loss, damage, or disruption caused by errors or omissions, whether such errors or omissions result from negligence, accident, or any other cause.

Ordering Information

Here's to Strong Women: Anthology II may be purchased in large quantities at a discount for educational, business, or sales promotional use. For more information or to request Ms. Stephanie Ford as the speaker at your next event email: info@getchamindright.org

Dedication

This book is dedicated to my two great aunts, Irene Johnson and Ada Banks, who outside of my mother, were two exemplary role models each in her own right. Through their class, style and grace, I learned what it meant to dress the part (literally) and how to mentally face life's challenges, handle them and show up in the world as the strong woman I am today. Both of my aunts gained their heavenly wings as this book was being written. I am blessed to have had them as examples of how to live life unapologetically as a strong woman.

To the tribe of women who have opened their hearts and minds to share their truths in the stories that follow, you too are examples of how to live life unapologetically as strong women.

Stephanie Ford

Stephanie Ford
CEO & Founder
Get Cha Mind Right, Inc.

"Here's to Strong Women. May we know them. May we be them. May we raise them."

Contents

I'M STILL STANDING

Eugenia L. McCaskill

Chapter 1

"Sometimes you must hurt in order to know, fall in order to grow, lose in order to gain, because most of life's greatest lessons are learned through pain."

~ Anonymous

I t's funny how the things in our lives that hurt us the most, are deeply embedded in our minds. Our memories shape our beginnings and our travels through life. I read something once from an Anonymous Author that states, *"On the road of life you must take the good with the bad, smile with the sad, love what you got and remember what you had. Always forgive, but never forget. People change. Things go wrong but remember the ride of life goes on."* Strange that I should remember that little poem, because I remember the events that I write about like they happened yesterday.

It had rained quite hard. The humidity that followed the downpour did nothing to cool the hot breeze flowing through my bedroom window that faced the back of the house. The bricks on the neighbor's house across the alley way looked like God himself had reached down and taken a wet brush, adding a fresh red coat of paint to the old bricks. Even as a young child, I was very outspoken. Whatever came up, came out. This time my mouth had gotten me into trouble. One afternoon my stepfather came home early. He was drunk as usual. He began to yell at me and did not like my response to him. He grabbed me and began to beat me. He continued to beat me until he could no longer reach me, as I ran up the stairs. The strikes were too numerous to count. I lay on the bed, my body in a fetal position, trembling inside. I lay there angry in sweat, tears and crying. I watched as the light mist of rain began to once again fall from the sky. The loud sound of thunder startled me, and I jumped, wincing in pain at the slightest movement of my body. I could still feel the sting on my legs and back. The welts on my arms were raised and visible from where I tried to shield myself and my face from the thick leather belt. He would often tell me that I was a bastard child. He told me I was nothing and I was never going to be anything. I was not his child and he didn't give a damn about me. I was young and I could not comprehend what the word bastard meant. I know that it was a word that did not describe me, and I was not going to own it. When he had been drinking or was drunk, anything I did (especially if he was angry with my mother) was an excuse to release his anger toward me. I lay there praying, "God please help me, help me please." I could feel the anger building inside of me. I wanted to fight him. I wanted to hurt him like he had hurt me. I really wanted to kill him. I lay there telling myself that this was the last beating, I'd had enough. No more. I swore out loud and I promised God that I would never let him beat me again. In an instant, I had made up my mind that if he touched me again, I was going to kill him. I didn't know what the consequences would be, nor did I care.

The Memories We Hold Dear

I was five or six years old. We lived on 16th Street between Columbia Avenue and Oxford Street in North Philadelphia. I don't remember staying with my mother much during my very young years, because she worked. However, I do remember my Chow dog named Toy. I also remembered living or staying with my Nana during the week. I probably stayed with my mom on the weekends, but I don't remember them. My Nana and Pop-pop lived in a small two-bedroom house on Stewart Street in North Philadelphia. I loved her with all my little heart and she loved me. She was not a very tall woman. I remember she always seemed to smell like Juicy Fruit chewing gum. I would later learn that it was to hide the smell of her shots of Seagram's Gin, she would sneak throughout the day. Her house was always immaculate. However, I don't know when she found time to clean, because it appeared like she was always with me. I would swear to this day that she never slept. When the neighbor's rooster crowed in the morning, she was already up and dressed and Pop-pop would be gone.

We would make the trek to Ridge Avenue almost every other day, to get fresh killed chicken and a few other items. The fruits and vegetables were bought from Mr. Jimmy (funny that I remember his name), who had an old broken-down horse pulling a wagon. Another man would be walking through the streets selling fish. "Shad, get your fresh Shad right here." We had an old ice box, that didn't keep food long.

I can still smell it; fish frying, country ham, fresh killed chicken, yeast rolls and the best doggone fresh pineapple coconut cake. Just kill me now! Yum!!! It seemed like she was always in the kitchen and the aroma of good cooking filled her little house.

Every morning after my bath and my breakfast, I plopped down on the floor between Nana's legs getting my hair combed and brushed. It was nothing fancy. There were just two or four braids and ribbons on each one to match whatever color dress that I was going to be wearing that day. Yes, I said dress, not jeans or pants. It may have been a pair of shorts with a midriff blouse, but mostly dresses. Before my little feet would find their way to the kitchen, Nana was up and making sure that my dress was starched and pressed. There was no such thing as spray starch, so she made up a small bowl of flour water and sprinkled the solution on my dress, while she ironed. I was more fortunate than most children my age. I had many dresses and two pairs of Mary-Jane shoes, a black pair and a brown pair. Just like we didn't have spray starch, she didn't have shoe paste to polish them up. Therefore, she would wipe them off with some lard to make them look almost brand new. No matter how hard I played the next day, they would always have a shine. They looked new again.

I was the golden child; the only child. My grandmother gave me almost anything I wanted. I was a little diva and I would often hear her say that "I was fresh as dishwater." I don't ever remember her raising her voice or even spanking me, except for one Sunday morning. I don't know where my Nana had gone. I was thirsty, and she was taking too long to come back and give me what I wanted. I took a bottle of beer out of the ice box and went outside on the stoop. I was still in my pajamas. I had my head thrown back with the bottle up to my mouth, trying to get a swig. From out of no-where, Nana appeared. She grabbed my arm and snatched my little butt up and smacked my bottom…" Lord Jesus child, don't let the neigh-bors see you with a beer, first thing on a Sunday morning." I didn't have sense enough or the know how to get the darn thing open. She had hurt my feelings more than my bottom. Some weekends when I didn't go home with my mother, my Nana, me and Pop-pop would get in his shiny black 1950 Buick. We would ride over to Lawnside, New Jersey, an area patronized by the *negro* community. I would be in the back seat, window rolled down and my head hanging out of the window, yelling "Pop-pop drive faster, so my hair can blow." With pigtails and ribbons blowing in the wind, he would always grant my wish. He would drive faster until my grandmother gave him the eye, fussing with dis-approval. I smile to myself every time I think of those days! They were happy times and un-knowingly they were going to change.

New Beginnings

Things did change. Although I couldn't explain it or understand it at my young age, I wasn't living with my Nana anymore. I was spending more and more time with my mother. I wasn't there that much, but she told me that we were moving from the apartment to a new house. I was going to have a new grandmother. My little head was swirling. What was going on? I didn't want a new grandmother. I wanted to go back to my Nana's house.

The new house was on a small street not far from Nana However, it could have been miles away for all I knew. I thought the house was big, compared to my grandmother's small two-bedroom house. I don't remember her exact words, but she told me that she had gotten married and that her husband was coming to live with us. Husband or married, I didn't care because my little world was about to be turned upside down.

Soon after we had moved into the new house, I was taken to meet my new grandmother and grandfather. My new grandmother seemed nice enough. I noticed she had a stiff leg. Upon our first meeting she grabbed me, holding me tight and kissing me all over my face. My grandfather was a quiet man and never said much. Whenever we visited, I always found him sitting in his chair reading the newspaper or listening to the radio. He greeted me with a smile and a hug. My new grandmother was a quiet Christian woman and her teachings gave me an introduction to the church. Although I complained, those lessons would come to play a huge part in my life.

Being a Christian woman, I wasn't allowed to do some of the things that I did at my Nana's house. Dancing was okay, but beer or stealing a sip of my mother's beer or even sweet wine was out of the question. I eventually grew to love her just as much as my Nana. We spent every Saturday at my Granny's house. We would arrive sometime after lunch and would leave after dinner, when it was dark. I had my own little nook in the living room, where my toys and dolls were kept. That was my little area where I would have my cookies, milk and sometimes my lunch. I was too young to play outside alone and I was happy.

I enjoyed spending time with my new grandmother, who I called Granny. She loved me and treated me as if she had known me all her life. The fact that I was not of her son's blood didn't bother her, but children have big ears. One day while at play, when my mother wasn't around, I heard my stepfather and his sister talking. His sister didn't like that my mother had been married before and her brother had married a woman with a child. She let my stepfather know that she was not happy with the current situation. She didn't mistreat me, but I just felt she would have preferred that I was not there. Things were pleasant enough. I found out there was going to be a new arrival. My mother was going to have a baby. Wow, a baby for me to play with. I was very happy. After what seemed like forever, a baby girl came home from the hospital. She was going to be my baby. I wanted to touch her and hold her. On several occasions, my mother would remind me that she wasn't a baby doll. She couldn't ride in my toy stroller or go outside with me.

The house where we lived wasn't far from my Nana's. However, it may have been in another part of the country. I was too young to know or realize that she was only five blocks away. I didn't get to see my Nana much anymore, but life was good and I was happy. I no longer got to spend the nights or weekends at Nana's. Most of the time I was now staying with Granny and loving her just as much as my Nana. Although the baby was here, Granny showed no difference in my sister and me.

As we grew older, more time was spent at my Granny's and less with my Nana. Sunday was the Lord's day and off to church we would go. I learned things in my Granny's household that I didn't learn from my Nana. I am not saying that she didn't believe in God. I never saw her go to church and she sure didn't take me to church. My Nana was more of the party grandmother and my Granny was the laid-back Christian family-oriented woman. My mom even joined the church and my sister and I became active with Sunday School, Vacation Bible School, the Children's Choir and so on. We were a family.

My sister and I were fortunate and blessed, for we had it better than most children our age. Some families only had one parent with no jobs and they depended on government assistance to live and survive. My mother was a seamstress and worked in the garment district making children's clothes. She later worked at Joseph H. Cohen and Botany 500. When I was older, on Fridays I would sometimes meet her at work. The Botany 500 factory had a store on the main floor. One day, as my mother and I were leaving the building, there was a large crowd standing around. As we passed, I saw a man, who seemed to be glowing. I was pulling back from my mother, because I wanted to see what was going on. Mommy, mommy, look its Kojak! He turned hearing my voice. He had his signature lollipop in his mouth. Looking at me and my mother, he walked over to us smiling and said, "hello pretty." He was tall, larger than life and a real movie star. I thought that he was pretty, as he cupped my chin in his hand. I was grinning from ear to ear, as he reached in his pocket and extended a lollipop in my direction. I looked up at my mother, to see if it was okay to take it. She nodded with approval. I took the candy and we continued out of the building. "Mommy, with so much excitement in my voice," that was Kojak, wasn't he pretty Mommy?" Yes, she said but his real name is

Telly Savalas and he was handsome, not pretty. I didn't care. I got to meet me a real live movie star!

My mother was a whiz on the sewing machine and made most of our clothes. They looked like she had purchased them from the children's store. They were so nice. My stepfather worked at the Quartermaster, a government agency. I don't know what he did there. I just knew that's where he worked. We never knew hardship or what it was to struggle, since both parents in the household worked. If our parents were struggling, we didn't know it. We had a nice home, food to eat and nice clothes to wear. Our life was good.

Sorrow and Change

I had never known death. However, at the age of ten, my stepfather's mother, (my Granny) passed away from cancer. I knew that she was in the hospital, because she was sick. However, I didn't expect her to die. My heart was broken. I didn't know what it felt like to lose someone you love or the pain you carried inside. When my Granny died, it was like another person had taken over my stepfather. He changed and gradually his inner demons slowly began to surface.

The years passed and while we continued to visit my grandparents' home in West Philadelphia, it wasn't the same. My aunt and grandfather were there but I was never as close to them as I was to my Granny. I interacted with my aunt out of respect, but I knew that deep down inside she really didn't care for me.

Just like all the other neighborhood kids, I started school. I had to get up early, because my parents took my sister and me to the babysitters, before they headed to work. They later hired a woman named Miss Simms, who was a friend of my Nana, to watch my sister and walk me to school every day. She looked like a grandmother, but her jaw always seemed swollen. She smelled funny and always walked around spitting in a can. I later learned that she dipped (smokeless tobacco) snuff. I never saw her stuff her jaws. I just saw them after they had gotten swollen. Yuck!!! Miss Simms stayed with us until the school term ended and I was old enough to stay home and watch my sister. We were not permitted to leave the house or go outside to play, until one of our parents came home. My stepfather would always arrive before my mother. We had daily chores to do. If we didn't get them done, we were not allowed to go outside. I always made sure that everything was done, but my stepfather was never satisfied. I was made to stay in the house and look out the door. When the ice cream man came down the street, my sister got ice cream, while I was told I didn't deserve any. The differences in the treatment of my sister and I were starting to become evident.

One day my stepfather came home from work extra early. He had been drinking and stopped at the stairs. Before going up to lay down, he turned and stared at me. His eyes were a glassy red. His hand reached down and touched the front of my t-shirt, where my young breasts were starting to develop. I felt sick, as I looked away. "I don't like you," he said. Don't ask me for anything, not a damn thing you understand? I just responded with a soft yes. That was the beginning of the inappropriate touching and the trips to my bedroom, when my mother wasn't home. I felt dirty. I didn't tell my mother. I had done nothing to him. However, from time to time, I would hear heated discussions between him and my mother about the way he treated me. It seemed like the very next day, he arrived home early from work. He was drunk. I tried to stay out of his way by adjusting and making the best of the situation that my young life would allow. I looked forward to going outside in the evenings, but I was never allowed to venture from the front steps. I didn't care because I was out of the house and away from him.

"Therefore, do not worry about tomorrow, for tomorrow will worry about itself. Each day has enough trouble of its own."

~ Matthew 6:34

Years passed and my relationship with my stepfather was just co-existence. I stayed out most of the time. I spoke when spoken to and interacted only when he initiated it. I was in my last year of elementary school and my Mother had taken a part-time job. This gave her just enough time to come in to get her dinner and head back out. It was still early September and the weather hadn't started to change. Once my homework was done, I was still able to go out and sit on the steps with my friends. I had been given a key and was old enough to come in from school and start to heat up dinner and start my homework. When I came in, my stepdad was home. I could tell he had been drinking. He seemed to drink every day. He gave me orders to get dinner heated up and to get my homework done. My mother came in shortly after dinner was done. My heart would be lifted, whenever she came home from work. Deep within, I was hoping that this would be one of the nights that she would be too tired to go to her second job. She ate, said her goodbyes and left the house.

I sat at the kitchen table reading a comic book and eating my dinner. I could hear my stepfather's footsteps above my head, pacing back and forth. Shortly after my mother had gone, he came downstairs and demanded that I fix him a plate. Doing what I was told, I hurried into the kitchen to fix his plate, so that I could bring it to the table where he usually sat. I did not hear him, but he had followed me into the kitchen. When I turned around, he was upon me. The back kitchen had been converted from a shed to what now held the sink, stove, a cabinet and the washing machine. It was very narrow, and I could not get around him. He had exposed himself. He grabbed my hand for me to touch him. I pulled away and I began to cry. He tried to undress me, almost ripping my blouse off me. I dropped the plate and fought him with everything that was in me. He slapped me across my face. Grabbing me around my neck, he dug his fingernails deep into my flesh. With me struggling and pulling away, he pulled a piece of skin out of my neck. My sister had been playing outside with her friends. When we heard her coming into the house, he released his grip and gathered himself together. I ran past him and my sister up to the bathroom. He had pulled the skin from the base of my neck and it was bleeding, hurting and stinging, all at the same time. I was so afraid and shaking that I wanted to run away. His touching had been going on for a while. How was I going to tell my mother? What was I going to tell her? Would she believe me? I could hear his voice talking to my sister, as I continued to hide in the bathroom. I poured cold water on my wound, until the bleeding stopped. It was a big gash with nothing showing, except white tissue inside. I was still hurting and shaking. I had no band-aid to put on it, so I left it open. I sat in the bathroom for what seemed like an eternity, until my sister came upstairs saying she needed to use the bathroom. I came out saying nothing, as I passed my sister and went into my room. As darkness fell, and not turning on any lights, I got myself ready for bed. I heard him when he came up the stairs and stood in the doorway of my bedroom. My back faced the doorway and I never turned to look at him. He knew that I was not asleep. He approached the bed, running his hand under the bedcovers. My body stiffened as his hand continued up my nightgown between my legs, touching my genitals. He leaned in close to my ear, telling me that I'd better not tell my mother or else he would get me. He turned and left my room. I was afraid to move and wet the bed, as I lay there trying to comfort myself.

When my mother came in from her second job, I had drifted off to sleep. I didn't see her until the next morning. My stepfather told my mother that I had gotten into a fight the night before and one of the girls that I had been fighting with, had ripped a piece of skin out of my neck. Of course, she believed him. My mother never questioned me or examined my wound. Showing no sympathy, she said, "serves you right." I was hurt, but it was like she didn't care. How could she care not knowing the real story? The usual morning conversations went on, before I left for school with my neck, sore, throbbing and hurting.

I met up with my best girlfriend. We walked to school together every day. I had never told anyone about what was happening to me. I told her that I had something to tell her. I made her swear and promise that she would not tell anyone. I told her in detail what had happened and had been happening to me. Her first question was, are you going to tell your mother? I said no, and she wanted to know why. She told me I need to tell her. I knew that she was right, but I was afraid. We walked to school together for the next two days and each day she would ask me if I had told my mother. My stomach was still in a ball of knots. Each day that I walked into the house, fear just took over. I was afraid to breathe. I became unclean. I wouldn't wash my body. I would use the bathroom and not clean myself when done. I prayed that this would dispel his advances and make him leave me alone. On the third day, as my girlfriend and I walked to school she asked again if I had told my mother? I said no.

We continued to walk in silence. My friend and I were in the same classroom. As soon as we got settled, without even raising her hand, she went up to the teacher. She was almost crying, as she talked to Mrs. Matthews. I saw the teacher raise her head and look in my direction. After promising she would not say anything she had told. My girlfriend walked back to her desk and Mrs. Matthews got up and made a call from the phone on the wall. I could feel the tears rolling down my face. When Mrs. Jacobs, the school counselor, walked into the classroom, she escorted me out. My heart was beating so fast, I could hear the pounding in my head. She took me straight to the nurse's office, where the nurse examined my neck. She walked away from me, having a discussion with the counselor. They both tried to calm me down. I was crying so hard; I didn't hear anything that was said. The counselor was going to call my mother. I knew that I was in trouble. What was going to happen to me?

The Truth Would Not Be Told

That night, I was called into my parents' bedroom. My mother was sitting on the side of bed crying. My stepfather started in on me, "Do you see what you have done to your mother? The lie you told the school counselor has gotten completely out of hand." I was crying just as hard as my mother. I tried to tell her that I was telling the truth. I don't even know if she heard me. I went back to my room.

The next day was a Friday and my stepfather went to work. I stayed out of school and my mother stayed home from work. She didn't question me. We never talked about what had occurred the night before.

"As children we are taught that it is a sin to tell a lie. Unfortunately, the truth does not always set you free."

~ Genie M.

The next day was Saturday. My aunt, my stepfather's sister, came to the house. She wanted to talk to me. She wanted to know why I would tell such a hurtful and vicious lie on her brother. I knew that anything that I said in my own defense wouldn't mean anything, because who was going to believe me? It was his word against mine and I knew that he had made his case very well against me. My mother sat there, listening to me as I spoke. My aunt was asking all the questions and I answered truthfully. However, of course, I wasn't believed. I was taking it out on my stepfather, because he had punished me by giving my sister money for ice cream and did not give me any. I was told that I had made up this hurtful lie, because I was being punished. I was crying, as I answered. I told the truth. I had no reason to tell a story. I was not believed. Everyone believed the wound on my neck came from a fight with one of the neighborhood girls. I had not gotten into a fight with anyone.

Several weeks passed and the dust had settled from the incident. My stepfather remained in the home and life went on. The tension between my stepfather and I was evident, but he never touched me again. His anger was taken out on me in other ways. I was now in junior high school and I didn't go to school in the neighborhood. The feeling was that the schools in the white neighborhood were better with fewer distractions. I went to Tilden Junior High School in Southwest Philly. It was an Irish neighborhood, where blacks were not welcome.

The differences made between my sister and I were evident. While nothing was said to me around my mother, I knew that I was not one of his favorite people. My Nana lived within walking distance. She called me to her house one Saturday afternoon. I knew I was going to have a good day spending time with her. To my surprise, my uncle was there. He had been asking to see me. I always received love from him, and he always bought me nice gifts. He would often get items from the docks, where he worked. This time he bought me a nice leather jacket. It was a little big, but I would be able to wear it when I went back to school.

I spent almost the entire day there visiting with him and my Nana. My stomach was about to pop, because of all food I ate. When I finished my slice of sweet potato pie, I said my goodbyes and walked home with my leather jacket folded neatly under my arm. When I walked into the house, my mother and stepfather were sitting on the couch. I pulled the coat from under my arm, excited to show it off. My stepfather asked to see it, so I handed it over. He took the jacket and started ripping it apart. He stood up, as he continued tear it apart. When he finished, it was nothing but a pile of rags. He looked at me and I could see the hatred in his eyes. My mother protested, asking him why he had torn up the jacket. He stated that my uncle didn't send one for my sister, so I wouldn't have one to wear either.

I was hurt and speechless. I couldn't believe the words coming from my mother's mouth. The next time you'll go to your room and keep your mouth shut. Although I was told not to tell my grandmother, I couldn't wait to see her to let her know what he had done.

Most of my time was spent in my room listening to the radio, reading and playing with our dog, which I named Butch. I had my friends and could go out to parties with a 12-midnight curfew, which was adhered too or else. The tenacious walls came down, when one night while out at a party I got caught out in a snowstorm. I was at Broad and Ogontz. The buses had stopped running and I didn't have a way to get home. I was going to miss my curfew. I called home to explain what had happened. To my surprise my stepfather came to pick me up. I thanked him and we had polite conversation during the ride home. He said that he couldn't leave me out there, but I think that my mother asked him to go pick me up.

I graduated from Tilden Junior High and moved on to John Bartram High School, which was located right behind Tilden. Racial tensions were high. Every day was a fight to get home. I liked being in school more than I liked being at home.

I was now living in the 1960's civil rights era. The presence of police at school was evident. It seemed like almost every Friday all hell would break loose, as you fought to make your way home. Tensions were high at school, at home and in the streets of North Philadelphia.

One day as we sat watching the news, it was reported (August 1964) that the police had beaten a pregnant black woman. Riots broke out everywhere. It was like we were living in a war zone. We could hear people running. Some were being chased, while others were running through the streets destroying property. The businesses on Columbia Avenue and Ridge Avenue suffered heavy damage, with fires being set, broken window fronts and looting of the stores. The fighting and the looting went on for two days. The sound of guns being fired, sounded like bombs. We laid on the floors away from the windows and away from stray bullets that might fly into the house. The rest of our summer was spent close to the house. You either sat on the stoop or stayed in the house. So much was happening in the neighborhood that you didn't want to get caught up in any trouble happening in the streets.

Life In Our Household Was Livable

An unexplainable and noticeable change had come over me. I didn't bother him, and he didn't bother me. I kept myself busy with schoolwork and my social life outside of school. I had thought that my stepfather and I had found common ground. My sister used to stay in trouble with my mother. On this one rare occasion, she was on the receiving end of discipline from her father. My stepfather, in his anger while beating my sister, forgot about the family dog. Butch was our protector and nobody, not even my mother, could touch us when Butch around. While Butch was the family dog, I took care of him. I was his master. I heard my stepfather yelling at my sister. While protecting my sister, Butch bit him drawing blood. Immediately after being bitten, he turned his attention toward Butch and begin beating him. I was in the kitchen and did not stir, because I knew that my sister was in trouble. It must have been something, if her father was on her case. I was in the kitchen preparing dinner. The black iron skillet pan was full of hot grease, I dropped the pieces of chicken in the pan. The commotion was moving in my direction as my stepfather was chasing the dog. Butch ran into the kitchen and got behind me. My stepfather followed him into the kitchen, trying to reach around me to grab him. It was like he was attacking me. I fell into my stepdad with such force, that he stumbled backwards. After composing himself, he lunged towards me. Without even thinking about what I was doing, I stabbed him in his arm with a long-pronged fork already in my hand. He screamed in pain and I reached back quickly putting on oven mitts. I took the pan with hot grease and chicken, throwing it towards him. He stepped back, only catching a small amount on his upper chest and the splatter of hot grease from the floor. He continued making a fuss about the blood coming from his arm, as my mother came running from upstairs to see what was going on. My stepfather was slumped over, holding his arm and chest area and screaming that I had thrown hot grease on him. He told my mother to call the police, because he needed to go to the hospital. I stood there looking at him in triumph. I still had the fork in my hand, as I took three steps towards him. I could feel the tears rolling down my face and the hatred and rage inside of me wanting to continue stabbing him. I was in trouble but I didn't care. The beatings and all that he had done to me came rushing back into my head. I had promised myself that I was not taking any more beatings. While the attack was not towards me, I was not going to allow him to hurt my pet. No one hurts my pets.

Several police arrived. One car took my stepfather to the hospital. The other car took my mother, sister and I to the police station for questioning. My sister and I didn't have the best relationship then and still don't to this day. She sat there crying and angry, because I had stabbed her father. She's lucky I didn't have a knife. I probably would have stabbed him to death. I was 15 years old and a juvenile. While I wasn't held in custody, I did have to go to juvenile court. The courts looked at the incident, but my stepfather saved me saying that it was an argument that got out of hand between the two of us. I had to go for counseling, but I didn't serve any time in jail.

Tensions between my mother and stepfather were running high and had been for some time. My stepfather continued to drink, and he and my mother continued to argue. One night as we arrived home, we found the house was in disarray. Several lamps and chairs had been turned over, food had been taken out of the refrigerator and thrown on the floor. We could smell the smoke and then we saw the light from the fire. The doorway of the cellar was on fire. My mother quickly grabbed a bucket of water that I used earlier in the day to mop the floor and threw it putting out the flames. My stepfather had what my mother would later explain to me was the rams, which came from drinking. He set the fire went upstairs and had gotten in bed. If we had not come in when we did, he probably would have died in the fire. We didn't have a phone, so I was given some change to go the pay phone to call the police. He was arrested for arson but was released and given a court date. He came home angry, because he had been arrested. He had to spend the night in what he said was a nasty, filthy jail cell. I laughed to myself, as I heard him take at least six baths over the course of the day. Several weeks passed. He went to work as usual and his drinking continued.

Is This Karma?

I was up early on Saturday morning to get my chores done. My mother had a hairdresser appointment and when she got back, I wanted to be ready to go to the movies with my friends. The daily chore list was tacked to the kitchen doorway. I knew it by heart. I checked it anyway to make sure I had accomplished everything on the list. I didn't want to give my mother a reason to tell me that I couldn't go out.

I could hear my stepfather upstairs. It sounded like he was in the bathroom, sick to his stomach. I ignored the sounds coming from upstairs and continued with my downstairs chores. I was hoping that he would be done, by the time it was time for me to clean the bathroom. My sister had chores to do, but she took her time. She didn't care if she was done or not, by the time mother got back. I left her sitting in the kitchen eating breakfast and I started up the steps to clean the bathroom. The smell of vomit filled the air. Our small bathroom was at the top of the stairs and to the left. The door opened outward into the hallway. I was not prepared for what I saw. The toilet and the floor were covered in particles of food and red mucus that turned out to be blood. The stench was awful but the sight of the mess in the bathroom made me almost sick as well. I turned away, covered my mouth with my hand and slowly closed the bathroom door.

I started towards the stairs but changed my mind. I walked towards the bedroom, because I could hear him crying. He was laying on the bed in his pajama bottoms covered in sweat. His stomach was swollen. I stood in the doorway motionless. He was moaning, and I could see the pain in his face and his eyes. I ran downstairs to tell my sister about his condition. She ran upstairs. I went across the street to a neighbor's house who helped to get him down the steps into the neighbor's car and to the hospital.

They took him to the University of Pennsylvania Hospital. My stepfather was tall and thin. I had never seen a man with a stomach that big, unless he'd had a beer belly. My stepfather did not have a belly at all. My sister and I were sitting in the emergency room, when my mother arrived. My mother stayed at the hospital and the neighbor, much to my sister's dismay, took us back to the house. I was upset, because I was looking forward to going out with my friends. However, I knew that the seriousness of the situation was not going to allow that to happen. My mother didn't get back home, until late that evening. She told both my sister and me the gravity of his condition. My stepfather had *gangrene of the stomach and his kidneys* were starting to fail. His condition had manifested itself over time. The doctor recognized that the condition my stepfather was in, came from years of drinking. He told my mother that my stepfather must have had blood in his stools and his vomit for a while. However, in his drunken state, he would not recognize the problem and if he did, he ignored it and told no one.

His condition was critical. The doctor explained they didn't know what to expect or what they would find when they operated. The years of drinking grain alcohol had done serious damage to his body. The alcohol he consumed over the years was not filtered or purified, like the alcohol purchased in the liquor store. When cleaning I would always find small jars of a clear liquid, not knowing what it was. My mother told me anything to throw it away anything that I found. The alcohol came from his place of employment. It was used for other purposes and should not have been consumed.

"Let all bitterness, and wrath, and anger, and clamor, and evil speaking, be put away from you, with all malice. And be ye kind one to another, tenderhearted, forgiving one another, even as God for Christ's sake hath forgiven you."

~ Ephesians 4:31 – 4:32

My mother went to the hospital every day. She went with my sister on the weekends. I had no desire to see him or visit with him. I had no sympathy for him and felt that he was getting exactly what he deserved. Several weeks passed and my sister and I had gone to bed. I wasn't asleep, when my mother came into my room to talk to me. My stepfather had been asking for me. She thought that I should go to see him. My mother had never approached me about the friction between me and him. I would often hear her talking to him about me. She never said anything to me about him. She knew how I felt, without me ever saying a word. She thought that I should go see him, although I wouldn't be made to go. The decision was left to me. She wanted me to think about it. After my mother left my room, I had already said my nightly prayers. However, I got out of bed and got on my knees to talk with God. I asked him to help me clean my heart of the hate towards my stepfather.

I sometimes went to church with my girlfriend, that had told the teacher about me being molested. She attended Wayland Temple Baptist Church, which was within walking distance of where we lived. She had called and asked me the night before to attend church with her, but I declined. When I woke up the next morning, I had changed my mind and decided to go. I told her how my mother had come to me the night before and asked me about going to see my stepfather. I told her that I wanted to go but was having a hard time because of the way I felt about him.

The service started, and much to the disapproval of the lady sitting in front of us, we continued to exchange conversation and candy. The minister stood in the pulpit looking out over the congregation and began to speak. Somebody needs to hear this message this morning. *"How Can You Hate Your Enemies and Love God?"* What? He repeated the phrase two times. The third time he repeated the phrase, he asked, "How many people in this congregation am I speaking to this morning?" I almost fell out of the pew! The pastor was long-winded, but I knew the message sent by God was meant for me and I listened.

"If anyone says, 'I love God,' but hates his brother, he is a liar. For anyone who does not love his brother, whom he has seen, cannot love God, whom he has not seen. And we have this commandment from Him: Whoever loves God must love his brother as well."

~ 1John 4:20- 4:21

As I began to walk home, I could feel the anxiety building inside of me. I had already made of my mind that I was going to the hospital. My mother and sister had already left for the hospital. The closer I got to my destination, the tighter the knot in my stomach became. I was scared to death, but why? This man couldn't hurt me anymore. He couldn't do anything to me. However, I was still afraid to visit.

My mother and sister were leaving, when I arrived. I walked into the room and saw a frail, helpless, thin man lying on the bed. He was almost unrecognizable. He was hooked up to a monitor and he seemed to have tubes everywhere. He opened his eyes and I could see the surprise on his face. My mouth was dry, but I managed to get the words out. Hi Daddy. His eyes filled with tears and he said that he was glad that I had come. He wasn't really expecting to see me. I stood there, not knowing whether to feel sorry for him or continue to be angry. This man, the only father figure that I had known all my life, had taken so much from me. He motioned for me to come over. As I began to sit in the chair next to his bed, he said no, please sit here on the side of the bed. I had not been that close to him in a long time and I felt him touch my hand. I sat there looking at him and he raised his eyes to look at me. He spoke in a low, almost whisper-like voice. I had to listen closely to hear him. *"I'm so sorry I just want to apologize. I know it may be too late, but I'm so sorry for the way that I treated you. You didn't deserve any of it."* I watched the tears falling down the side of his face, as he continued to repeatedly apologize. I didn't speak, but I could feel my heart racing. My eyes filled with tears, as I watched him lay there crying for what he had done. He didn't blame me for the way I felt towards him, and he understood. I had heard words from my stepfathers' mouth that I thought I would never hear.

He broke the chains that had me bound. To heal within myself, I had to let go of the hatred that I had carried around for so long. I had been beaten, molested, degraded and told that I would never be anything. The pain and the hell that I endured, made me what to prove him wrong. I pushed myself to be the best at everything I did.

"Just as it takes a village to raise a child. It takes a village to abuse a child and everyone plays their role. Emotional abuse, emotional neglect, physical neglect, physical abuse and sexual abuse. You have the direct abusers, the secret keepers, and the people who blame and shame the victim. It takes a village to abuse a child."

~ Anonymous

Healing Through Hurt and Anger

My stepfather began molesting me, when I was seven years old until the age of fourteen. We had a secret. I was being controlled. I worried about how much it would hurt my mother and what would happen to me, if I told.

"Forgiveness doesn't excuse their actions. Forgiveness stops their actions from destroying your heart and the person you are meant to be."

~ Genie M.

Watch…Healing through the hurt when nobody believes you or ignores your cries for help is hard. **Look**…The expression of a child and their body language reveals so much, if you just pay attention. **Listen**…Parents listen to your children, every word that comes out of their mouths is not a lie. One and one has got to make sense when it adds up to be two. Child molesters **do not discriminate!** Don't be so damn in love with your significant other that you can ignore what is happening around you to your child or children, be they *male or female*.

When questioned my molester blamed everything on me. My story was made up because of his strict rules and the punishment that I received. I was not taken to a doctor and examined to see if I had been penetrated or received other injuries to my vaginal area. My injuries (a sprained wrist, bruised lip) that I received from him, were ignored because he said they came from fights that I had encountered while outside. They did not question any of my friends to collaborate anything that I said, and I was not believed. My relationship with my mother and sister suffered drastically. My molester, my abuser was not arrested and received nothing more than what I call a slap on the wrist. To protect him, his standing among family, friends, and his government job, he was made to leave the home.

"In my distress I cried unto the Lord and he heard me, deliver my soul oh Lord from lying lips and from a deceitful tongue."

~Psalms 120:1-2

Hatred hurt, and anger can destroy you if you let it fester. I found the power in my childhood prayers *"Now I lay me down to sleep, I pray the Lord my soul to keep"* changed to *"Lord help me to hold out."* I can do all things through Christ which strengthens me. I still carry a deep hurt, and a remembrance of so many things that should not have been, but I am vigilant, and I'm Still Standing.

DADDY'S BROKEN GIRL

Tia McNeil

Chapter 2

Dear Beautiful One,

I know it hurts and it may seem like a revolving cycle. You may be scarred but you're not broken. Take time to heal and love yourself for who you are. It's your responsibility to change the blueprint of your life. In case you needed a reminder, you're worthy and more than enough.

I see the Queen in You.

Growing up, I used to think that love was supposed to feel like a Disney movie. Boy, was I truly in for a rude awakening! How could something that's supposed to heal, cause so much pain and bring you down the most? That's the question I often asked myself. Instead, I was lied to and manipulated into believing this is what true love is supposed to look or feel like. I settled for men who gave me less than I deserved. I was mentally and emotionally abused for years. My feelings were often left for dead. Feeling overlooked and abandoned became the norm for me. I stayed in relationships longer than I should have, because this was all I knew. The hurt, pain and betrayal were deeper than my heart could take.

I've always had a loving and kind heart, so why would someone want to destroy me this way? I never imagined I'd be in situations like this and I didn't want the cycle to continue. There had to be another way, and this can't be the definition of true love. I'd watch couples on TV, thinking "That's exactly how it's supposed to feel"? I wanted that "Martin and Gina" kind of love" or "Heath and Claire Huxtable" kind of love. My only desire was to feel loved and protected. I never felt safe in love. My heart felt like it was held captive. Is it me? What am I doing wrong? Why do I allow them to treat me this way? Then suddenly a light bulb went off. That's when I realized that this pain didn't start with these men. I was familiar with being treated this way. This pain felt like home. I was comfortable there. It all started with the first man I ever loved. I fell in love with a man just like him . . . My daddy

Like some women, I was born out of wedlock. My birth caused a lot of pain and confusion. Prior to my mother, my father had already been in a long-term relationship with another woman. The relationship was rocky at times and they'd often "Break up to make up". During the time when he separated from his long-time girlfriend, my father went back to the dating scene and he eventually met my mother. My parents fell in love at an early age, were inseparable, and soon became pregnant with me. I always believed my father loved my mother the best way he knew how. However, he didn't love her the way she deserved to be loved. This is where the cycle began. My mother is the sweetest, most kind-hearted and loving woman I know.

She'd often put other's desires before her own. She poured a lot into those she loved, and she never gave up on people. Unfortunately, it backfired on her and things began to go left. Don't get me wrong, my father was always there for me physically but not emotionally. He worked hard and always made sure he instilled values and morals. However, he failed to cover me emotionally. My parents were on and off for years. After breaking up with my mother, he decided to go back to the other woman. When she found out about me, she was furious. She resented me and made sure that I knew exactly how she felt every chance she got. I was 10 years old and I called my dad's house, because I was excited to tell him about a stereo I saw in the store.

The woman answered, and I nervously asked, "Can I speak to my dad"? she said, "No!" and hung up abruptly. I immediately called back and asked for my dad again "Can I speak to my dad please" she screamed with rage, "He's not here," and proceeded to hang up the phone again. When I brought this to my dad's attention, he appeared to be enraged and told me he'd handle it. I felt at ease knowing he'd rectify the situation and walk away from the woman who doesn't accept his child. Weeks later, I asked if he had talked to her about the way she handled things. He stated, "Yes, baby girl I dung in her ass and I'll never let anyone else hurt your feelings again". However, I was wrong and he stayed. Once again, my feelings were swept under the rug and my emotions were left for dead. I started feeling abandoned.

Months later, my dad brought a house with this woman. They lived a few blocks away from my mom and me. I was never invited to his new home and I couldn't understand why. It seemed like she was his #1 girl and I was left to figure things out on my own. I'd bring this to his attention. However, as usual, my feelings were dismissed. I appeared to be overreacting. I couldn't wrap my mind around the fact that my father, the man who brought me into this world, would stay with a woman who hated his child so much. He allowed her to disrespect me and that was my biggest issue with him. My father told me he loved me every single day but he put this woman before his own child. He never left her, and I always felt like he protected her more than he did me. I allowed him to disregard my feelings and we just moved on in life, as if nothing ever happened. When I became an adult, things began to click, and my vison got more clear. I had questions and I started demanding answers from both him and my mom. I became even more inquisitive and irate. I was no longer just going to sit back and let things slide. Someone was going to answer my questions and that's when all hell broke loose.

My grandfather became ill in 2010. My dad asked me to join him on a trip to South Carolina to visit him in the hospital. I agreed to go, and I was excited to spend time with him. We had a nine-hour drive ahead of us, so there was a lot of time to talk and connect with each other. We talked and laughed the whole ride down. I thought, "This feels great." I always wanted a close relationship with my father. I looked forward to our bonding time. I enjoyed being around him. His sense of humor is unparalleled. When we arrived in South Carolina, things

weren't looking good with my grandfather and his health declined rapidly.

My dad was extremely close with his parents, so I knew this was tearing him up inside. I tried my best to comfort and console him to keep his spirits high. However, I couldn't help but notice the "shiny" ring sitting boldly on his ring finger. My anxiety began to rise. However, I kept my cool for several reasons. This wasn't the right place or time to say anything. I knew that if I addressed it, my feelings would be ignored. I'd again appear to be the angry, broken, bitter daughter that I've quickly become. Days went by and I said nothing. I thought, "there's NO WAY he married this woman". Feeling perplexed and confused, I kept these feelings bottled up. I contemplated how I was going to address this issue. My dad was still seeing my mom on and off. I didn't want to get her involved, because I knew this news would destroy her. I needed facts and I was determined to find out the truth. I prayed and asked God to give me a loophole and lead me into the

conversation. And he did JUST THAT. Later
that evening after leaving the hospital from seeing my grandfather, my dad was eager to show
my grandmother and I a video production he
had just started working on. He brought a new
video camera and he was practicing his videog-
raphy skills. Filled with excitement and thrilled
to show us his work, the video slowly started
playing. There was a family and they all seemed
to be laughing and enjoying each other at a gath-
ering. I didn't recognize anyone in the video, the
house they were in, the artwork on the wall or
the voices that seem to be filled with joy.
Shortly into it, was when I saw HER. It was the
woman he chose over me. Without hesitation, I
said tensely, "Dad, who the HELL are these people" He looked at me in shock and said, "This is
XXX and her family." I stormed out of the room.
I asked him to meet me in the living room, because I didn't want my grandmother to know
what was going on. At this point, it was "no
holds barred". If he was bold enough to show
me her and her family, I was going to be bold
enough to say what was on my mind. I instantly
asked. "Are you married to this woman"? He
said, "No". I looked down at his hand and

pointed out the ring on his finger. I asked again, and he proceeded to lie to me and answered heatedly "No, Tia". Something didn't feel right. The vibe was off. I knew in my heart that what he was telling me wasn't the truth. I went back in the room with my grandmother and I told her what was going on. To my surprise, she already knew who this woman was. Eventually, it came out that she also knew that he married her without telling anyone. It was just a matter of time before my mom and I found out. I started screaming at the top of my lungs, "You're a fucking liar and I hate you." He then admitted he was married to her by "common law" In that moment, time and hour, I felt like I had lost my dad forever. I looked at him with rage in my eyes and told him he would never see me again and he no longer had a daughter. I walked out of the room and called my mom to tell her what I discovered. I could hear the tears coming down her face and the pain in her heart. She hung up the phone, speechless. I wanted to go home and hold my mommy, but I couldn't because I was so far away. Heading back home, after leaving my grandparent's house, we had a nine-hour drive in complete silence.

The man I once knew, was the man who no longer existed to me. Two months later, my grandfather passed away. Funerals and weddings always bring families together, so I wasn't looking forward to this moment at all. I hadn't seen or talked to my father, since the incident happened. He often called, texted and left voicemails expressing how sorry he was and that he should never have let this happen. I ignored every call and text. Shortly after my grandfather passed, my grandmother died unexpectedly. I knew this would push him over the cliff. He lost his parents back to back and then his daughter. The Bible says, "Honor your father and your mother, that your days may be long in the land that the Lord your God is giving you" (Exodus 20:12).

I truly believe this scripture and my conscience led me to reach out to him. We didn't speak at my grandmother's funeral. His woman never let him leave her side. She stood by him, like a soldier sitting in the ceremony with dark shades on. He tried to embrace me but I wouldn't let him. He was heartbroken and left feeling lost and abandoned. I knew this feeling all too well, so I put my feelings to the side. I grabbed my daddy by the hand, took him outside and started praying for him. For the first time ever, I started to understand what it meant to love someone unconditionally. I loved him through my brokenness. This is when reconciliation began to take place. Life hits us hard sometimes and it's not always fair. From this experience, I've learned that I'm much stronger than I thought I was. Being strong isn't always easy. Never let anyone diminish your value, just so they can be comfortable and happy. You matter, and your feelings are also valid. We often don't speak up or say what we feel, out of fear of losing the ones we love. Everything that's meant for you will eventually make its way to you. Don't hold back, sis. You may be scarred, but you are not broken.

I can't control what happened to be during my childhood. However, as adult I am responsible for my healing. I refuse to go through life feeling bitter. I've been stuck in relationships, where I've been cheated on, lied to and mentally and emotionally abused. I thought this is what love looks like, because I saw it in my daddy so much

What you allow, is what will continue. I could no longer accept and allow people to treat me badly and devalue me. I am a daughter of a King and I deserve to be loved the same way God loves me.

I was raised in church, so I knew God at an early age. Years later, I started to realize that this was a cycle and I didn't want to become a slave to it. I found God and I started praying. I prayed and asked God to help me see myself the way he saw me. "Ask, and it shall be given you; seek, and ye shall find; knock, and it shall be opened unto you" (Mathew 7:7). I was no longer afraid to walk away from people, who couldn't see my value. I love my parents with everything in me. I'd do anything for either one of them. My dad and I speak every day. However, we don't discuss the issues of the past anymore. I've forgiven him, which is why I'm able to live a happy, bold and free life. He's made me the woman I am today. I am powerful, ambitious and driven. I will never give up on true love.

I've been doing a lot of soul searching and the 'Inner work" it takes to overcome my issues. I love God, people and my family. My circumstances don't define me. I know that one day I will find the love of my life and I will be mentally and emotionally prepared to give him the very best of me. God isn't through with me yet.

What is Love? 1 Corinthians 13:4-8 tells us,

"Love is patient, love is kind. It does not envy, it does not boast, it is not proud. It does not dishonor others, it is not self-seeking, it is not easily angered, it keeps no record of wrongs. Love does not delight in evil but rejoices with the truth. It always protects, always trusts, always hopes, always perseveres. Love never fails."

At some point, I had to stop using at the trauma caused by others as a crutch and do some soul searching. I had to dig deep and identify the root of my pain. I couldn't control how others treated me in the past. However, I knew I had to take ownership of my toxic ways and begin healing. Fighting depression at an early age, being abandoned and feeling broken made me stronger. I know it's easier said than done, but you must keep fighting. Fight to heal, grow, love, but most importantly, fight to be a better you. On the journey to becoming your higher self, you will face many challenges, but you must do the inner work. Do what you need to do to get to a healthy mental space.

It all starts with you.

Do the "heart work" and your relationship with everyone around you will change.

#WON'T SHE DO IT!

Yes, I Did And Yes, You Can Too
My Journey Towards Conquering PCOS

Denine Kirby

Chapter 3

"We can do anything we want to do if we stick to it long enough."

~ Helen Keller

The Pink Stuff

In color psychology, pink is a sign of hope. It is a positive color that inspires warm and comforting feelings. Pink represents the sweetness and innocence in children. It also

represents our inner child. It is the color that
symbolizes uncomplicated emotions, inexperi-
ence, and naivety. Pink can also take us back to
our childhood memories, which are often associated with the care and thoughtfulness
received from our mothers or another maternal
figure in our lives. Pink makes us feel that everything will go well.

I loved the pink stuff! As a child, I had
frequent stomach aches and given the pink stuff
to tackle the pain and ease the discomfort. I
loved everything about it — the color, smell, tex-
ture, thickness, temperature, and taste. I
particularly liked the smell (the smell reminds
me of Icy Hot), and even now I have an emotional reaction to the smell of muscle pain-
relieving and sports rub products. I know it is
odd, but I digress. The creamy, warm-colored
pink stuff and its minty, chalky, liquid thickness
oozed downward and coated my throat and
tummy. It would soothe my pain in more ways
than one not only physically but also psycholog-
ically, spiritually, and emotionally. My Mom
kept the pink stuff in the refrigerator, so the temperature was always perfectly chilled. I always
felt better after each spoonful. I felt more secure

and supported after each dose. Sometimes, I asked for it because it was necessary to calm my chronic stomach aches that resulted from eating foods that did not agree with my body. Other times, I had more of a psychological and emotional need for the pink stuff. It eased some of the uneasiness or stress that I experienced, which often manifested as my "tummy ache." Sometimes, I would fake a stomachache because I needed some extra attention. I also loved the ritual interaction between my mother and me, which often happened at bedtime and sounded something like, "Momma, my stomach hurts." Momma would knowingly ask, "You want the pink stuff?" to which I'd excitedly reply, "YES!

"Okay," Momma would sweetly answer. Then she would open the refrigerator and pick the bottle up from the door. I could hear the suction release, as she closed the door. I could also hear the clank of the utensils, as she grabbed a spoon from the drawer and closed the drawer door. There was a sliding sound and then a small thump. She'd open the cap, pour me one spoonful, feed it to me, and then give me another dose if I asked for more.

"Thank you, Momma," I'd whisper to her as she tucked me in.

"Now go to sleep," Momma would say, "I love you."

The entire ritual soothed my soul, quieted my anxiety and fear, and alleviated my upset stomach. It gave me much of what I needed at that moment. As a child, I was not sophisticated enough to acknowledge and articulate these feelings. In those moments, all I knew is that I experienced stomach aches and that the pink stuff, and the way Momma gave it to me, made me feel better no matter what.

In retrospect, and regardless of whether my symptoms were a result of a physical, psychological, or emotional need, or any combination of the three, (and I suspect this was the case), Momma's ritual always worked. Momma always provided relief, regardless of my reason for needing it. What is the "pink stuff"? For some, it's described as Pepto-Bismol Digestive Medicine. For others, it's called the Bubblegum Medicine, but for me, the pink stuff was my Comfort Medicine.

The pink color has a calming effect on our emotional energies and can relieve feelings of anger, aggression, and neglect. Pink helps people get in touch with their thoughtful and caring side, either through the need to receive, give or care for others. Please pay attention if you have a friend who often wears pink, as it may indicate a need to be accepted, supported, and loved.

My First Set of Mystery Symptoms

As an adolescent, during one of my medical appointments due to my irregular cycles, I asked my doctor why I had so much gas. After I ate most of my meals, I would experience gas and bloat. I was always bloated, even though I had a very small 110 lb., 5'4" frame. My body was small and lean, but my stomach protruded. I constantly looked as if I was pregnant. Not giving it much thought at first; I just thought that was how I was made anatomically and that there was nothing I could do about it. I surely never connected my bloated stomach to the foods I ate, and apparently, neither did my doctor. He did tell me to stop drinking carbonated drinks while I was eating. Therefore, he was half right in giving me that advice as a solution. The fact of the matter is that it is not the best practice to drink any liquids, carbonated or not, at the same time as you are eating. Drinking beverages while eating does not allow for nor facilitate proper digestion. The doctor never explored my issue any further. He did not ask any other questions to dig deeper, and he did not explore what could be the underlying problem.

My Second and Third Set of Mystery Symptoms

It was a lost opportunity for awareness and possible diagnosis. Unfortunately, the doctor's information was not more insightful when he attempted to explain my irregular periods. I was told that having my period every three months "might be normal" for me. When I was told that I might only have a period a few times a year, I knew instinctively and inside my gut and my heart of hearts that the doctor's explanations were erroneous. No! Having my cycle every quarter or two to four times per year was just plain wrong. However, at that phase, in my health journey, I was naïve and vulnerable. He was the "expert." He knew best. He knew my body better than me, or so I told myself. Therefore, I took what he said as gospel. I trusted the information given to me. I accepted the information about my body without further curiosity or inquiry. I was always forced to be prepared because it could come at any time and under any circumstance. There was no pattern to track. My cycles were all over the place. They would come without warning and stay with me for days during some months and weeks at a time during other months. There was no pattern, no predictability, no purpose, and no white pants! As a young woman, I was secretly happy that I did not have to worry about my period. There was no period every month. Wow! Yes! I celebrated this fact until I was prescribed and began taking the birth control pill.

Around that time, I also learned that my sister faced similar challenges symptoms such as acne, irregular periods, and more. Her symptoms were explained away because she was an athlete. I was no athlete so we could not possibly be experiencing the same things for the same reasons. Uh no! Not possible! Just plain WRONG!

As it turns out, from the tummy aches that led to Momma easing my upset belly with the pink stuff, to my very sporadic menstrual cycle, there was a very valid reason for all the issues that I'd faced thus far and explanations to all the forthcoming issues that will arise soon. And it has a name -- Polycystic Ovary Syndrome, also known as PCOS. And it is likely possible that PCOS runs in the family genetics.

Please allow me to take this opportunity to introduce myself to you. My name is Denine La Tawn: I am the third child and baby of the family born to Franchotte and Ella Marie Webb Nalls. I have two older siblings, Dennis La Monte and Denise La Vonne, ten and eight years my senior. I was raised in a suburban neighbor-hood in Carson, California (Los Angeles County). My dad was hard working and pro-vided well for his family. My mother worked when she wanted to. My Mom was and still is very resourceful. She was a very big influence on my upbringing. She was my protector, my teacher, my role model, my friend, my advocate and most of all my mother. There was nothing she would not do for her children. She was fear-less! She was my complete opposite! As a young child, I was small in stature, and my personality was quiet and introverted, introspective and non-confrontational. I did not like loudness, yelling or screaming. I hated when anyone was mad at me for any reason. I liked to keep the peace. I was the "good girl." I was a girlie girl. I did not climb trees, get dirty, play rough, speak loudly, or cause trouble. I did not bother anybody. I was well-mannered, well-behaved and liked overall by others. I was friendly and kind. I had many childhood friends. I was a happy child and enjoyed life. I was a good student and a good citizen. I know that I was wanted, and I felt loved by my parents, siblings, family, neighbors, church family, and community. Some may even say that I was spoiled. I lived my life outwardly "in the pink!" Inwardly, I was living my life, "seeing red."

One day (I was in high school by then), I just started crying uncontrollably for no apparent reason, and I could not stop. My Mom came into my bedroom, where I was lying on the bed. She tried to talk to me by asking me what was wrong. I replied, "I don't know." She was extremely concerned and did her very best to soothe me. Momma hugged me and held me tight and close while trying to talk to me to discover (unsuccessfully) the source of my pain and tears. Then she prayed with me. She prayed until I slowly calmed down and was able to stop crying and regain my composure. This scenario was out of the ordinary for me. That experience is like a snapshot in time. It's a part of my history that I will never forget. I could not articulate what I was feeling. Intense feelings of sadness overwhelmed me. I think my Mom finally summed my episode up to being normal teenage hormones and growing pains. Unfortunately, this was simply the first of my episodes of this intense sadness.

My Fourth Set of Mystery Symptoms

A very important point that I want to make here is this: Parents, please listen to your children! Pay attention to the small, subtle clues of stress and anxiety that your children may experience. I know hindsight is indeed 20/20, and I don't blame my Mom in any way for not recognizing the signs. Remember that our personalities were complete opposites. The signs of my challenge presented very differently than the way they may have presented in others who were dealing with pain, like what I had. My signs were all internal. I showed my stress and anxiety by sucking my thumb. Sucking my thumb was a habit of mine until I left home for college. I was passive and fearful. I ate very little, showed low frustration, experienced chronic stomach aches, and was not able to identify and articulate how I was feeling. I had no words. I could not use my voice.

One impact of childhood traumatic stress can be long-term health problems, such as diabetes and heart disease. You can add PCOS to this list. I share this part of my story with the hope that you learn from my experience. Hopefully, your road to wellness is not as hard as mine.

"In the middle of every difficulty lies an opportunity for growth."

~ Dalai Lama

During childhood, adolescence, and as a young adult in my twenties, I was petite, thin, and healthy overall. I'd always had a

protruding stomach. Eventually, I just rational-
ized it as an anatomical defect. I've always had
struggles with irregular menses and digestive
problems, to the point that I normalized these issues. However, when I turned 30, all hell broke
loose! My body began to change and change
drastically. First, was the weight gain for no apparent reason. There were five pounds here and
five pounds there. By the time I reached 38, I
weighed over 200 lbs.! Generally, I had a healthy
diet, so I could not explain the fast weight gain.
I was gaining weight primarily in my midsection, which was of concern. I then noticed that I
felt terrible after eating certain foods, especially
bread. After eating bread, my belly would swell
terribly. The bloat was unreal. It was as if I
baked the bread in my gut! There was no need
for an oven. It was unpleasant. Another symptom was acne. I'd never experienced acne during
my teenage years. Therefore, to start having
acne after age 30 was frightening. I am talking
about severe cystic acne all over my face, fore-
head, cheeks, jawline, and chin that left scaring
to underscore its presence. As if that was not
enough, my husband, Jimmy, noticed dark,

black patches on my neck. He called it "the black neck."

I always was a worrier. I lived with anxiety since I was a very young child. However, with my body changing as rapidly as it was, the changes were causing my anxiety levels to increase. I felt fatigued, out of shape, and grew very self-conscious about my appearance. No matter how supportive my husband was in trying to assure me that everything would be okay, he was secretly also very worried about me. He even clandestinely talked to my Mom about the changes he was seeing in me.

During the decade of my 40s, I began to experience pelvic pain, especially after intercourse. I grew more facial hair (hirsutism) and then began losing my hair on my head. My hair was thinning at the temples of my head, and I was starting to see male-pattern baldness. Oh NO!

Help me! I used to scream with terror from within. I think I am changing into a man.

"Thank you, Sir!" My head quickly was on the swivel to observe who might this kind, but an uninformed person was and who were they addressing. Then, I heard it again, "Thank you, Sir! Have a good evening." My heart sank as I heard these kind and enthusiastic words directed at me. There was no one else around, so I was forced at this point to come to the uncomfortable, shocking, and utterly horrible realization that his clerk was talking to me! Unfortunately, this was not the first time I was mistaken to be male. It was not the first, nor would it be the last. After this encounter, with tears in my eyes, I asked my husband, "Do I look like a man? Do I look like a man? How could he have mistaken me for a man? How is this possible with these size G breasts on my chest? Why?" How?" Although this was not the first time that had happened, at that moment, it was the first time I was so hurt and confused.

More Mystery Symptoms

Do you know that the average woman sees at least five different health care providers before given a diagnosis of PCOS? My journey is a bit different since I diagnosed myself with the help of a television program.

"If you want to go fast, go alone if you want to go far, go together."

~African Proverb

It was the year 2005. Jimmy and I were living in Ithaca, NY. "This is me! That is me!" I screamed, "That is me!" as I watched TLC's program, *Mystery Diagnosis*, featuring Ashley Levinson. She told her story of her symptoms and struggles with the disorder called Polycystic Ovary Syndrome or PCOS. That segment had originally appeared in Season 2; Episode 5 and was entitled, *Why Is Emily Screaming?* It aired on Oct. 14, 2005. I frantically searched for anything to write on and took as many notes as I could regarding this mystery. I turned to Jimmy and said, "I have to get to Philadelphia to see this Katherine Sherif, MD." Dr. Sherif is a leading PCOS Practitioner who started treating women with PCOS, and in 2000, she established the country's first academic program for Polycystic Ovary Syndrome. My symptoms are no longer a mystery! Ashley was me, and I was her. All I needed at this point was confirmation.

August 2007, moved to Philadelphia.

It just so happens that the trajectory of our lives presented the opportunity to make Philadelphia our home. For my husband, it was professional, and for me, it was personal. I was now one step closer to meeting Dr. Sherif! And who would have thought that I would also get the opportunity to meet Ashley?

April 2008, brother died.

I dedicate this writing to my one and only brother, my BIG brother, Dennis. He died at the age of 48, the same age that I am now writing my story. My story is synchronous with his. It is cyclical. However, this is the moment it stops. The buck stops with me! Let the cycle be broken! It all ends here. He died in his sleep from heart failure due to diabetic complications. He battled with his health for a while. Sadly, he went into a diabetic coma and suffered sepsis shock. He lost his leg, his kidneys failed (he was on dialysis), and he had degenerative vision loss. He paid the ultimate price with his life. I hope his transition was peaceful during his sleep. My father also died of a stroke due to high blood pressure, five years earlier in 2003. I am now faced with a decision.

May 2008, first day of work at Temple University.

As a condition of hire, I had to take a physical exam. The provider put me on the scale and asked me if I wanted to know my weight. I hesitated because this was a new experience. No one had ever asked me if I wanted to know what the scale read, and I had never felt reluctant to know. I then replied, "No, I'd rather not know." I followed up with, "Is it over 200 lbs.?" She said, "Yes." I wanted to cry. To this day, I do not know what that scale measured. I do know that it was the heaviest I had weighed in my life.

October 2008, the tipping point.

In my hand, I had a recruitment brochure for Improving Health and Maintaining Weight Loss Through Telemedicine research study at Temple University's Center for Obesity Research & Education (CORE). The purpose of the study was designed to compare the effectiveness of two different approaches to long-term changes in weight and health. They were looking for overweight men and women to participate in a community-based lifestyle program to promote moderate weight loss and increased physical activity.

Working in medical academia, I always enjoyed participating in studies and being a "subject." I was a sort of human guinea pig to help researchers prove or disprove their hypotheses. Since I was always principally healthy, I felt as though I was contributing to both the medical profession and society at large. My participation made me feel as though I was single-handedly empowered to help society.

In this spirit, I eagerly signed up for a research study (CORE) that was looking for subjects who wanted to lose weight. They were investigating a new telemedicine program to test the hypotheses of which group would be more successful in weight loss: the group that met for in-person support groups once per week or those who only met online.

To be considered, I went through a complete physical that included a three-hour blood glucose test. This is where my journey began! At the end of this process, my lab results showed that I was hypertensive and pre-diabetic. This news hit me squarely between my eyes, across the head, and pierced me straight to my heart. I had just lost my brother six months earlier from diabetic complications. I cried as I replayed my brother's struggles of injecting insulin, the slow loss of his sight, low immune function, constant battle with infections, such as necrotizing fasciitis (flesh-eating disease), septic shock, amputations, kidney failure, dialysis, heart disease, and death.

I was devastated! I was hurt! I was terrified! And I was driven! I was determined! I was ready! I was committed! I decided that this was NOT going to be me. I WAS NOT GOING OUT LIKE THAT!

July 2009, I was over 200 lbs., hypertensive, and pre-diabetic.

It took over one year to get an appointment to see Dr. Sherif after my health insurance started, two years after moving to Philadelphia and three years after seeing *Mystery Diagnosis*. But it was all worth the wait. Dr. Sherif spent over an hour with me getting a thorough background medical history, listening to my fears, concerns, and goals while offering a wealth of information and support. She understood that I wanted to reverse this condition with minimal pharmaceutical intervention. I wanted to reverse the symptoms with my food choices, exercise, and lifestyle changes. She said, "Yes, you can." She gave me the tools and the push to do just that. She offered alternative therapies, rather than the traditional birth control pill and metformin. She offered inositol and berberine as options. She provided guidance and resources on nutrition, stress reduction, a support group, dermatologist and psychologist. Armed with my confirmation diagnosis of PCOS and resources, I was ready to fight.

So, what the heck is PCOS? What was I fighting?

PCOS stands for Polycystic Ovary Syndrome. Polycystic ovary syndrome, or PCOS, is the most common hormonal (endocrine) syndrome affecting up to 21% of patients in some countries. PCOS is a serious lifelong genetic, hormonal, metabolic, reproductive disorder that affects 1 in 10 women (over 10 million) worldwide. Many associate PCOS as reproductive simply due to symptoms like irregular periods, cystic ovaries, and the most glaring issues of infertility and miscarriage. It is the leading cause of infertility based on ovulation dysfunction. It tends to be the only symptom and age group; some doctors care to treat!

PCOS is more than a reproductive condition. It's a metabolic and endocrine syndrome, PCOS has the potential to affect every organ system, if not properly managed can lead to future health issues like diabetes, stroke, sleep apnea, hyperlipidemia, and heart disease, to mention a few (sounds familiar? childhood traumatic stress). The National Institutes of Health estimate that more than half of women with PCOS will become pre-diabetic or diabetic before age 40 (yep that was me! I was age 38). Some studies have found that PCOS sufferers are three to four times more likely to develop endometrial, ovarian, and breast cancers.

Despite impacting millions of women, PCOS is unknown to most people. An estimated 70 percent of the women living with PCOS are undiagnosed. PCOS is a lifelong syndrome that is not limited to age, and there is no cure despite claims pregnancy, ovarian drilling, hysterectomy, and menopause. Although these may offer symptom relief, they only typically address reproductive issues and not the endocrine system or underlying cause.

Some symptoms include:

1.   Weight gain

2.   Belly fat/ Bloating

3.   Facial hair

4.   Tubular breasts

5.   Acne

6.   Skin tags

7.   Thinning hair

8.   Dark spots on skin

9.   Low sex drive

10.   Mood swings

11.   Anxiety/depression

12.   Insomnia/sleep apnea

13.   Sugar cravings

14.   Pelvic pain

15.   Irregular menstrual cycle

16.   Insulin resistance / diabetes

17.   Infertility

18.   High cholesterol

19.   High testosterone

20.   Fatigue

PCOS is a syndrome that manifests itself with its host of symptoms with the root cause of hormonal imbalance, dysfunction, and/or disruption. It involves a vicious cycle of hormone imbalance. Approximately 80% of women who have fewer than six menstrual cycles per year also have PCOS.

Your "thyroid is the battery to your body." It drives the metabolism of every single cell of your body. Hormones are made by the thyroid gland. They control EVERY function within our bodies. If we control our hormones and if we can get all our hormones in check and balanced, then we will not experience the symptoms associated with PCOS. My priority is in managing this syndrome. I strive to feel, look, and live my best life, regardless of this diagnosis. My goal is overall health and wellness (physical, emotional, mental, and spiritual).

October 2009, certified group fitness instructor.

I could not have done this if it was not the support, guidance and cajoling from my co-worker, Ms. SS. I am forever appreciative for what she has done for me. By this time, I was also successful in lowering my testosterone from my original level of 113 ng/dl down to 37 ng/dl. The normal range for adult females is between 8-60 ng/dl. I had enough testosterone for two adult women! I accomplished this first goal of reducing this hormone by walking during my lunch breaks at work and eating fewer carbohydrates and less sugar. At this point, I had not eliminated anything from my diet; I just decreased my portions and increased my exercise.

I am happy to share these ten tenets and action steps developed during my journey. Working the action plan helped me to achieve my goals. I am the conduit of my purpose! Following these ten guidelines, is how I fought and how I continue to fight! And how you can start to fight too!

Self-Care for Reversing PCOS and its Symptoms

1. Think and visualize yourself as having the health you want, desire, and deserve. Repeat this act of mindfulness daily. Take out everything that pulls you away from your objective and your intention of vitality, fitness, and well-being.

2. Write affirmations to support your health goals. Recite these affirmations at least twice daily. Reduce resistance, resignation, and cynicism. YOUR BODY FOLLOWS YOUR MIND; CHANGE YOUR MIND; CHANGE YOUR BODY. Are you ready to change your DNA?

3. Trust your body. Track your body. Keep a journal of your symptoms. Track your weight and any other necessary measurements, i.e., blood sugar, blood pressure, etc. Write down what you eat and record how your body and mind feel after eating those foods. This exercise will help you develop your individual and specialized eating plan to include foods that are

good for you, make you feel good and provide for you with the energy/fuel you need daily.

4. Get right back on track after you've temporarily gotten off. Practice following through having fun and being resilient! Instead of giving up, acknowledge the breakdown, take responsibility, forgive yourself, learn the what, why, and how from experience and keep it moving! Don't give up!

5. Find one professional who listens to you and is knowledgeable about PCOS (or is willing to do the research and learn alongside you).

6. Develop your plan of action. Stay in the present. Be patient with yourself and remember that your desired health outcome manifests in small increments. Just start where you are now.

7. Find a support group. The African proverb states, "If you want to go fast, go alone if you want to go far, go together." You don't have to do this alone. Why would you want to? The journey to health and wellness is easy and fun if you make it social and supportive.

8. Get out of your comfort zone! Give yourself a challenge and make it measurable. Do something that feels illogical to you at this moment. For me, it was planning to run the Philadelphia Marathon and participating in a triathlon. Find your challenge and sign up for a 5K and 10K event in your area.

9. Exercise with female friends. Socialization is the cornerstone of wellness. Participate in as many wellness programs as you can. Movement is key!

10. Be your own health advocate. In all things, seek vitality, well-being, and fitness. Exercise your personal power and free self-expression. You are the expert of your body. I want you to know that no matter what runs in your family or what genetic makeup you have, you have agency over your own body, mind, and your health. You can change and live your life so that those genetic markers do not express how you show up in the world nor affect your life at all.

CHANGE YOUR DNA - CONTROL YOUR GENETICS – YOU CAN GET WELL, HEAL YOUR CELL.

The True Genesis

I'd always thought that my PCOS journey began at age 30 when I started to notice the unique and unmistakable changes that began to occur in my body. However, upon reflection, I realize that is false. The stories I shared with you about my early childhood and adolescence regarding the Pepto Bismol and my inconsistent cycles demonstrate that I had been battling PCOS for a very long time. I was just not aware of what was wrong, and obviously, neither were my physicians. I have been experiencing PCOS symptoms throughout my entire life. First, as a very young girl with digestive issues and anxiety and then in my puberty years with irregular menses, mood swings, anxiety and hirsutism, and as an adult with food sensitivities digestive issues, weight gain (particularly around my midsection), acne, hirsutism, insulin resistance, high blood pressure, depression and infertility.

"Success can be measured not only in achievements but in lessons learned, lives touched and moments shared along the way."

~ Nishan Panwar

Someone once told me that my story was not for me. It was for other people to whom you share. You live your life and have your set of experiences not solely for you, but for others in which to witness, learn, gather strength and inspiration. You don't have to always learn the hard way, by making your own mistakes. You can learn from others' experiences. By sharing your story, you can show others that they are not alone, to prove that there is a silver lining and life on the other side and to find commonality and community.

In the past, I felt that participating in conversations with people was cumbersome, exhausting, and quite simply a waste of time. I simply did not like it! I did not like it because I always felt as if I would be exposed. It required a level of vulnerability that I was not willing or able to give. It required trust and faith in people that I did not possess. It was hard!

Thank goodness I no longer have these same feelings. I now approach each interaction with people (regardless of how I truly feel at that moment, trust me I resist heavily sometimes) as an opportunity to share, learn, connect and be curious. I always take something valuable away with me after the conversation. Now, I am free to be bold, open, vulnerable, exposed, and to give what I receive. Don't get me wrong; it takes tremendous energy. The difference now is that I practice generosity. Interaction is no longer a waste of energy/time. Energy is neither created nor destroyed. It is only transformed or transferred from one form to another. I simply get what I give, and it is truly wonderful.

I am Not Going Out Like That: A Decade of Transformation

"Life is a grindstone. Whether it grinds us down or polishes us up depends on us."

~ Thomas L. Holdcroft

For the last decade, since receiving the confirmation of the PCOS diagnosis, I have been on this journey of health and wellness. Each step I have taken on this journey has led me toward learning more, helping more, expanding my social networks and growing more. I began this journey to heal from my medical conditions; then I began to help others to achieve their goals as a group fitness instructor and exercise coach. My desire to serve, my professional training, and personal strengths have all allowed me to find my place in the world. My Mom told me that I was born to be a healer. I have always been very resourceful. I am a good listener, and I am empathic. Others have described me as resilient and affable. I believe that my strengths, my personal motivations to help and inspire others, and knowing my passion/place in this world to do work that is meaningful, impactful, and supports others, has led me to this place in my life and my life's work. I aspire to inspire, motivate, support, and push others toward their wellness goals. I have information, love, and care to offer to my community. I was forced to advocate for my health. I now advocate for others who find themselves in my story.

My life circumstances became my story, and my story became my inspiration for transformation!

Now I stand before you victorious!

I am NOT overweight. I am NOT hypertensive. I am NOT diabetic.

As a group fitness instructor, exercise coach, and health and wellness professional, I live, demonstrate, and teach awareness, as well as the process of taking responsibility for improving and maintaining your well-being. How did I get here after a decade of struggling, experiments, breakdowns, and breakthroughs?

It took me ten years to finally reach my goal weight and to produce a perfectly good bill of health. There is now no more diabetes, no more high blood pressure, and no high testosterone. I now know my body and what foods I can eat to give me optimal health without bloating, without gas and digestive challenges. My acne is clearing, my hair on my head is thick and healthy, and the hair on my face is unnoticeable. I can identify and soothe my anxiety. Authentic appreciation comes out of completion. I am complete! I choose daily to create authentic appreciation!

This series of 10 is very present to me. It speaks to me. It nudges me. The number ten symbolizes the completion of a cycle.

Get a Personal Cheerleader

I can now continue this journey and advocate for other women who find themselves in this same struggle. As the owner of **Delna Wellness**, I have many instances where I make meaningful connections with people along their health and fitness journey. Ms. T's goal was to qualify for weight loss surgery. We worked together without judgment, and she successfully reached her goal. She was and is still very grateful. This procedure changed her life, and she is still doing well after three years of keeping a healthy body weight. As an exercise coach for older adults, I make an impact by simply keeping my word. Ms. C appreciates my calls. She has very little family, and she doesn't have many visitors and callers. Therefore, I make sure to call on her consistently. I hope that this has made an impact on her life. She now comes to class consistently and has expanded her social connections. She even tells me that she is no longer lonely.

I am approachable, a good listener, and non-judgmental. I suspect that this is the reason why people enjoy talking to me and will confide in me. This past Saturday, Ms. W told me that she is struggling financially and is worried about losing her business that she has worked hard to maintain for the past three years. She told me that she had not told anyone about her situation. She just needed to tell someone to get it all out, so I listened. I am honored that she trusted me enough to share such personal details. Afterward she felt better, her stress level declined, and she felt heard. This is how I impact others daily, in small, but meaningful ways.

One of my clients, Ms. D wrote:

"You speak to our spirits; you challenge our souls to want better, and then you push our bodies to do more. Impacting our path and changing our thinking. Continue to walk in your authority, healing yourself and being an example for others to heal themselves too."

To create the space for transformation and to open the possibilities for women to see themselves as powerful, healthy, happy and whole is my life's work, purpose, and mission. In 2015, I created **Delna Wellness** to provide the tools, information, resources, community, and support needed to choose health and wellness

ALWAYS....to rediscover your personal worth...to reclaim your personal power. I stand for these women, even when they can't see it for themselves.

Through **Delna Wellness,** transformation is achievable with movement, nutritious and delicious food choices, creative wellness and mindfulness, in an environment that is social, supportive, easy and FUN.

"When you move your body, mental and physical strength develops, confidence grows, and transformation manifests throughout all areas of your life! It is your Divine right to be well, healthy, and whole."

I intended to share my story and to take you on my journey. I hope that you will hear something that will educate and inspire you so that you, too will share your story of transformation. I did not accomplish these breakthroughs on my own. I am truly grateful to my physician, Dr. Sherif, for all her knowledge, care, openness, patience and guidance throughout this fight. I am grateful for my husband, Jimmy, for his unconditional love and support and for having a blind eye, just at the right times, and for always being my cheerleader. I am grateful for my brother, Dennis, for inspiring me to fight and for this opportunity to continue our life's work. I appreciate my mother, Ella, and my sister, Denise, for loving and encouraging me and changing their habits, only to support me. I thank all my family, and especially my fitness family, for growing with me, for encouraging me to be and do better, to be an example, shining light, and for pushing me to be my best.

We Need Your Help!

Polycystic ovary syndrome (PCOS) is the most common hormone disorder in adult women. Although there is no cure, this condition can be effectively managed. Although many treatment options are available for the multiple aspects of this condition, remarkably, so little research has addressed the quality of life and psychosocial issues that frequently accompany a diagnosis of PCOS. I hope that this writing will call more attention to this critical unmet need for women with PCOS. We need more evidence-based treatments. We are desperately in need of more information. We need to learn how to lessen some of the more troubling symptoms, and we need to help collect the evidence for the therapies we propose, by supporting the appropriate clinical trials.

Support H.Res.495 and S.Res.336

PCOS Challenge: The National Polycystic Ovary Syndrome Association worked with Congressman David Scott (D-GA-13) and 20 other leaders to introduce resolution H.Res.495 in the U.S. House of Representatives. PCOS Challenge also worked with and Senators Elizabeth Warren (D-MA), David Perdue (R-GA) and five other leaders in the U.S. Senate to introduce S.Res.336.

PCOS Resolution S. Res.336 passed by unanimous consent in the United States Senate on December 21, 2017, recognizing the seriousness of polycystic ovary syndrome (PCOS), the need for further research, improved treatment and care options, and for a cure for PCOS. They also designated September as PCOS Awareness Month. This historic and bipartisan effort represents the first time there has been a central focus on PCOS in the U.S. Congress. H.Res.495 has attracted more co-sponsors than any other health resolution in the 115th Congress.

To move H.Res.495 forward and out of committee, your representatives need to hear from you and your family to understand why PCOS is a critically important issue. As a constituent, you have a powerful story to tell about your own experience with PCOS or that of someone close to you. Thank you for helping to change the future for millions of women and girls with PCOS.

Three Quick and Easy Steps

Step 1
Find your Congressperson by entering your zip code and address at http://www.house.gov.

Step 2
Check to see if your Congressperson is already a co-sponsor of H.Res.495

If your Congressperson is NOT already a co-sponsor of H.Res.495, please personalize the Word document co-sponsorship template letter at https://pcoschallenge.org/cosponsor-draft-letter.docx

If your Congressperson is already a co-sponsor of H.Res.495, please personalize the "thank you" template letter at https://pcoschallenge.org/thank-you-draft-letter.docx

Step 3

Email your personalized letters to advocacy@pcoschallenge.org or fax them to PCOS Challenge at (301) 244-9902. All letters will reach your Congressperson's office.

For additional information and resources regarding PCOS, please visit the following websites:

PCOS Challenge: The National Polycystic Ovary Syndrome Association is the leading 501(c)(3) nonprofit patient support and advocacy organization globally that is advancing the cause for women and girls with PCOS serving over 50,000 members.

https://pcoschallenge.org/

PCOS Awareness Association is a nonprofit organization dedicated to the advocacy of polycystic ovarian syndrome (PCOS). The organization and its dedicated volunteers are raising the awareness of this disorder worldwide, providing educational and support services to help people understand what the disorder is and how to treat it. The Association also provides support for people diagnosed with PCOS to help them overcome the syndrome and decrease the impact of its associated health problems. We are a registered non-profit organization dedicated to the advocacy of Polycystic Ovarian Syndrome (PCOS) that occurs in over 10,000,000 people worldwide.

https://www.pcosaa.org/

To find a study on PCOS, seeks out CenterWatch. Founded in 1994, CenterWatch is a trusted source and global destination for clinical trials information for both professionals and patients. Located in Boston, CenterWatch provides patients unbiased information on clinical trials along with health and educational resources.

As a pioneer in publishing clinical trial information, CenterWatch was the first Internet site to publish detailed information about active clinical trials that could be accessed by patients and their advocates. Today, they have one of the largest clinical trial databases actively seeking patients on the Internet.

https://www.centerwatch.com/clinical-trials/listings/condition/313/polycystic-ovarian-syndrome/

As part of this journey to wellness and freedom from PCOS, I found my calling, my passion, my why, my reason for being here on this earth during this time, and space. My entire life is about helping everyone to secure and maintain health for themselves! Being healthy is indeed the greatest possession on this earth. There is nothing better than having good health. I am here. I stand for you and with you, by sharing what I know. Together we can grow and move forward in our own personal health voyages to secure, regain, and maintain optimal health and wellness. Let's do this together!

For support and more information on how I am "fighting like a girl," please contact me at Delna Wellness. I am also available to book for speaking engagements, training, and coaching in the areas of health and wellness, PCOS advocacy, hormonal health, food choices, and self-care. I can be reached as follows:

Phone: 267-225-7389
Email: delnafitness@gmail.com
Websites:
https://www.facebook.com/denine.kirby
https://www.facebook.com/delnawellness

Here's to YOU, my strong sisterhood. Cheers to YOU, strong women. Fight Like a Girl – PCOS Awareness!

HIDDEN WOUNDS

Lucress Irizarry

Chapter 4

"The wound is the place where light enters you."

~ RUMI

LuLu in the Light

She was a teenager with light skin and dark brown hair. I was about seven years old at the time, so she stood much taller than me. She was not a part of my family, but she was trusted enough to be assigned to me as a caregiver. She used to take me to the corner store to get some of my favorite snacks, like chico sticks, green apple Now and Laters, LG potato chips and Tastykake Krimpets. We would come back to my mother's house and watch TV or play a board game. Sometimes, while we were watching TV, I would sit between her legs on a huge pillow, while she would braid my hair. I really enjoyed getting my hair braided, because she would create these very pretty designs with the beads that I picked out from one of our trips to the corner store. I looked and felt very pretty with my colorful beads, that were held in place with foil at the tips of my braids. I felt like an African princess, especially when I would swing my hair back and forth. I would hear the sound of my beads and smile a big happy smile with my big dimples. My hair coupled with a twirling skirt, my lace ruffle socks and white patent leather Buster Brown shoes, made me feel like I was the most beautiful girl in the whole wide world.

I was Lulu in the light. I was carefree. I believed that I could do and become anything. I loved everyone around me, especially the women in my life. I knew that I could trust them. I never questioned their trustworthiness or the trustworthiness of other women that I encountered. I thought that every woman could be trusted because my mother, grandmothers and all the women in my family, knew how to treat me, love me, care for me and protect me. My friend loved and cared for me to the extent that she felt like family and I trusted her implicitly.

We had so much fun together! She was my best friend. Sometimes she would take me for extended walks around the neighborhood, to the park to swing, play hopscotch, play board games or jump rope. There were times that we had so much fun that I grew tired from playing so hard. When we returned home, I would gently fall asleep to the TV. Everything was good, lovely and true. Life was a beautiful dream.

Shadows in the Light

It was a particular summer day in 1985 that was like none other. The soap operas had just ended and the game shows like Press Your Luck and The Price Is Right were starting to play. The TV was turned down low and as I was falling asleep, I could hear the quiet screams and applause from the audience on the game shows.

We had so much fun that day, like we did every day. I took a nap to recharge. I laid on the floor pillows to take a nap, because it was much cooler on the floor than on the couch. To my surprise, I woke up to her lying beside me in a spooning position. I did not think that this was out of the ordinary, because my mom and dad would cuddle me in this manner when I was younger. It was a loving touch.

The loving touch then turned into a weird touch. It was a dark touch. She pressed her fingers into my private parts. It was the place where no one, except my parents and the doctor was allowed. It was a strange touch. It was unfamiliar. It felt good, bad and WRONG all at once. I said NO. I told her to STOP. She whispered, "shhhhh, everything is OK. It's OK. It's OK. It's OK." She kept pressing into me, while she was telling me that it was okay and to be quiet. I kept quiet, because she was my friend and I trusted her. I didn't cry out, but I really wanted to, because I felt violated. I felt dirty. I felt ashamed. I felt helpless. I felt alone. I felt like I was slipping away from the moment. I didn't understand what was happening to my body.

My heart was racing. I was afraid. Confusion set in, as I was engulfed in silent terror. She continued to press into me and pulled me toward her. She held me tighter and tighter, until we both began to shake.

After that day, she committed the same heinous act a few more times. I remained silent. I never told anyone. She said that if I told, we would both get into trouble. Time passed. Seasons changed and after a while, I never saw her again. I don't remember what she looked like in detail. I don't remember her name. All I remember was the void she created, that was once filled with my innocence. There was a wound in my heart, where the love for my "friend" was lost. She was the thief that stole my innocence and the victimizer that committed sexual abuse against me.

It happened again among other children, with a teenager leading the pack. They took advantage of the girls, who were much younger and defenseless. I was at a neighbor's house after school. My neighbor was known for having a nice space for children to play in her home and provided adequate caregiving services. There were three other girls in addition to me. They were acting like they were in church service and catching the Holy Ghost. The teenaged girl would then act like she was supporting one of the younger girls, who was acting out the part of a churchgoer in the spirit. She would press her crotch into her backside, while holding the girl's vagina tightly until both of the girls started convulsing. The teenage girl caught me in a similar manner, by cornering me and pressing herself onto my backside. I couldn't get away, because she was much taller and much heavier than me. I was helpless. None of the other children helped me, because she was larger, and they were afraid of her. I didn't tell an adult, because I was also afraid of her. If I told, I knew for sure that she would beat me up. It never occurred to my childish mind, that maybe if I told someone I would have been removed from that unsafe, toxic environment. Maybe if I told someone, she would have been exposed and prevented from doing this shameful thing to other children. Maybe if I told someone, she would have gotten help from a therapist to learn how to understand her actions and how to think differently. I felt even worse, because I was not brave enough to speak out. I felt guilt and an internal conviction regarding the fact that I didn't protect myself from this happening again.

I realize now that the teenage girls who were violating younger girls, were only doing it because someone did it to them. The fact that those girls were victimizing other children was a form of retaliation. They were victims who were robbed of *their* innocence. They were angry about it. Somehow, they thought that taking away the innocence of other children in the same manner, balanced the scales of injustice.

Much later in life, I discovered that what I experienced was a form of sexual abuse, known as molestation. I coped by not sharing it with anyone and stuffing it deep down inside the depths of my heart. I built a wall of rejection, sarcasm, coarse joking, defensiveness and deflection. I disengaged myself from the pain and shame, like a bullet discards its shell once it leaves the gun chamber. There was no need for it. There was no need to acknowledge it and certainly no need to share it with anyone. It happened and then it stopped. And that was all...or so I thought.

The Evidence of Things Not Seen

The events passed but the evidence of a wound still remained overgrown and hidden by a scab of painful truth mixed with happy sadness. I used my smile with my deep dimples to hide my wounds. I thought that if I just smiled a great big smile with all of my love shining through my brown, starry eyes, then no one would ever know how much I was hurting inside. I learned very early in life that if I spoke well, behaved in an acceptable manner, studied and excelled at school, the adults around me would never question if there was anything wrong with me and I would never have to provide answers. I was taught at a very young age that my word was priceless and would lose its value, if I ever broke it. As a result, I didn't tell anyone for fear of losing the love and respect of my parents, family and friends. I, therefore, engaged my intellect and used the energy of my pain to excel in my academics, because I knew that if I concentrated and did well in school, then I would not have to think about the shame and guilt that I was feeling just below the surface of my success.

Underneath my bold smile and confident exterior, I felt guilty about being involved in an immoral act. The realization and consciousness of that act caused me to feel the weight of shame. I questioned how I could feel guilty when I was the one who was molested. I should have felt nothing but anger. However, instead I felt like I was just as bad as my abuser, because I violated myself with my silence. I betrayed my own trust, which made me feel worthless. I felt like my self-esteem was on empty and a deep sadness had begun to set in. I thought that if I can't even trust myself, then what is the point of my existence and purpose?

I questioned why didn't I push her hand away again and again? Why didn't I struggle harder to get up? Why didn't I kick and scream? Why didn't I write a simple note to my parents about what happened? Why? Why? Why? I now know that I did none of these things, because no one really had in depth conversations with me about the possibility of something like this happening to me, so obviously no one told me that I should tell someone even if they threatened me. It was still a time when the world seemed innocent and neighbors loved each other as they loved themselves.

I now understand that I was a child with a mind that did not understand how to think critically to consider the full consequences of each action and reaction.

I didn't have conversations about sex and sexuality, until I was well into my teens. What my parents didn't realize, is that those conversations should have happened much sooner. However, I don't blame my parents because I know that they did everything they knew how to do to protect me. They protected me the way that their parents protected them. For the most part, I lived a very sheltered life and they did not expose me to just anyone without vetting them first. My parents were still cautious around the people who were vetted, especially concerning me, because they lost a son to illness prior to my birth. When someone new came around our family, they had to earn their trust and be around for a long time before being accepted as extended family.

War Cry, "No!"

My family used to complain about me frequently saying the word "no.". I initially thought that the only reason was because my Dad, who primarily raised me, taught me to say, "no" by saying it to me so many times. That was only part of it. I now realize that I say "no," because part of me is still that wounded little girl who never spoke out about what happened and that is her way of fighting back. It is an echo of what she silently cried out, when she was being violated.

My "no" was the action that I took to try to snatch back the power that was stolen by the enemy of my soul. The enemy who used a teenage girl to rob me not only of my innocence but my confidence, self-esteem and ability to speak the truth without shame. My "no" was a war cry to reclaim my freedom from the chains of guilt and shame. However, my "no" was not the salve for the wounds created by my oppressor.

My "no" was just a band-aid at best. It was a weak attempt at trying to heal myself. It didn't restore that part of me that was devastated and ruined. My "no" was being used improperly and was fertilized like a crop of bad fruit.

Bad Seeds, Bad Fruit

My feeling of shame manifested itself in different ways. The seeds of self-defeating thoughts fell onto the fertile ground of my mind and dug deep roots, to the extent that it became the fruit of my belief and a pillar in my paradigm.

I believed that I was ugly, because, like the girl who touched me and all of those other girls inappropriately, I was a female. I believed that they were ugly. I believed that all girls were mean and could not be trusted. I believed that those girls who touched me were bad. Sadly, I concluded that, since I was a female like they were, that I must be bad too. I became very cautious and very apprehensive around women. I didn't want to hug women with a full embrace, because I didn't want them to think that I wanted to be intimate. My hugs, therefore, would be a light hug with one or two arms, without other parts of my body touching. I never wanted to be around girls who were fast and fresh. To protect myself, I stayed inside my home, read books and watched television. The only real conversation or interaction that I had with girls was at school where there was adult supervision at all times. I realize that my limited interaction with girls, is the reason why I didn't have many girlfriends.

I was uncomfortable undressing in front of girls in the locker room. I made sure to change my clothes inside of a bathroom stall. I learned how to change my clothes, without revealing any of my undergarments or my nakedness.

Being sexually abused has also partly contributed to my perceived disdain for public speaking. The same fears that I developed from being sexually abused are the same fears that came up every time I had to speak publicly. I was afraid to speak because I thought that I would get into trouble and people would laugh at me, call me names and ridicule me. I would think that no one would believe me. They would think that I was a liar. If they thought that I was a liar, then they would always question me about whether or not I was telling the truth about everything that I said. I had a dysfunctional belief that my credibility and integrity would be compromised if I spoke to large groups of people.

When opportunities to speak were presented, my heart would begin to pound to the point where it felt like it was going to jump out of my chest. It was so bad that I could feel it in my ears, and I couldn't move because I was literally paralyzed by fear. I felt like I was dying. This was the defining moment that made me realize that I had to get serious about doing the work on myself to start healing.

Empowered Healing

My healing began, when I accepted the fact that I was molested. My healing grew when I spent time with God in prayer and meditation to discover that he does not condemn me, because I believe in Jesus Christ. I discovered the truth of the fact that God loves me, and He came to give life, so that I will have it abundantly.

I acknowledged that experiencing the feeling of good and bad feelings simultaneously, while being sexually abused, was a natural response to being touched. The healing continued, when I forgave the teenage girl who snatched my happiness, security and protection. The healing further progressed, when I forgave myself for not being strong enough to protect myself and for being too weak and afraid to tell the truth about what happened. My final stage of healing lies within the words of my pain that you are reading because I am sharing them with you. The validation of this is in the word of God that states "we overcome by the blood of the lamb and the words of our testimony." (Revelation 12:11) This is my testimony.

Once I decided to uncover my wounds and allow them to heal from the light and air, I realized that I did not have to keep carrying the burden of sexual abuse. My faith in God carried me to the life-giving water of God to be healed in mind, body and soul. The Bible says, "come unto me all ye who labor. And I will give you rest. "God invigorated me with His light, so that I could be blessed today.

Break the Cycle

I am sharing my story to raise parents' awareness about children being molested by other children. When the seed of oppression is planted and begins to take root, it often bears the fruit of an oppressor. As a result, the viscous cycle of sexual abuse continues. This is why it is important to develop trusting relationships with your children, so that the "awkward" conversations about sex, sexuality and similar topics become easier.

Don't rely solely on the schools to educate your children about sex. Teach them about good touches and bad touches, as soon as they are able to speak. Inform them about who is allowed to touch them and where they are allowed to touch. Empower them with the words that they can use to let someone know that they are uncomfortable with how they are being touched. Expunge any worries they may have about speaking to you as their parent or another trusted adult, because they think that they will get into trouble or be accused of doing something wrong.

Spend time with their friends, the parents of their friends and anyone who their friends' parents associate with, who may visit their friend's home. Play dates are fine during the day. However, be careful about whose home you allow your child to go to for a sleepover. Try to minimize harm by either participating in the sleepover or hosting the sleepover at your home, so that you can keep a close watch over your child and their friends.

Pay close attention to your child and any behavioral changes. If you are not paying attention, you may not recognize the subtle differences in their behavior. For example, before being molested, I was a free spirit and I trusted people. I felt safe and I loved to go outside and spend time with my friends. After I was molested, I became a home body, who stayed in the house often. I did not want to go out and spend time with my friends. I just wanted to read books and watch TV. I developed this protective habit to the extent that I still do the same thing as an adult. As a result, I can become distant and cut myself off from networking and getting to know some really great people. It has affected how I engage with people, which is why networking is not my favorite thing to do. I am working on being comfortable with networking, because if I don't then I won't continue to mature socially, and my business will suffer.

Parents don't dismiss your child, when they tell you about the abuse. Listen to them and confront the person who did it. Be proactive and practice what they can say and do, if someone tries to abuse them sexually. Have a dialog and in some cases, role play how they should respond if someone tries to force them to do something that they don't want to do. Explain what sexual abuse is in a way that they can understand. Explain that sexual abuse could involve someone touching them or the abuser asking the child to touch the abuser's genitalia.

There is a verse in the Bible that talks about a thorn in Paul's side and is the part where Jesus says, "My grace is sufficient for you, for My strength is made perfect in weakness." (2 Corinthians 12:9). This meant that He wasn't going to remove the thorn in Paul's side, so that he would remain humble and not become conceited in all of the greatness that God had put into him and was now birthing out of him for the edification and the deliverance of the people of God -- Christians. Paul was sharing this in the Bible, because there are things that were great within him and he did not want to become prideful and conceited because of them. I believe that there is greatness inside of me. It took me a long time to realize this truth about myself, because I believed the lies that were planted by sexual abuse. Understanding this truth about myself has helped me to become the strong confident woman that I am today. However, before that I was very introverted. I still am introverted but now there is a voice for my introverted self. I express myself through writing books, speaking to audiences and coaching clients to break free from the chains of their past, in order achieve the dream goals of their future.

Like Paul, the thorn in my side is the sexual abuse that I suffered. It was my cross to bear, so that I could share this story with other people, women, parents and girls. I speak out so that they may know that there is healing and deliverance and that they don't have to carry the

• 118 •

shame and guilt that comes with being a sexual abuse survivor. The truth is that the wounds that we bear were made to allow the light to shine through and melt away bitterness, anger and shame. When those negative emotions fall away, what is left is the light of love and the amazing transformation that takes place to become a new creature, who will make a difference in the world.

THE LISA HANSON STORY

Lisa Hanson

Chapter 5

I am the epitome of someone who does not look like what they've been through. I have survived, and have even learned to thrive, through circumstances that would at best take the joy, if not the life, from others. So many women have lost their lives. I am still here. Not only am I still here, but I am still full of hope, joy and love. In this chapter, I share a number of select vignettes – true, dramatic, crazy stories from my life. My prayer is that you would glean life-changing lessons and strength, as you read some of the things that God allowed me to endure. My hope is that you believe, from reading my story, that if I could emerge victorious from a life that challenged me in the way mine has, that nothing can stop you from finding your way out of whatever is also testing you.

I Forgave Them for Me

I want to make it clear that I honor my mother and my father. When I refer to my parents or say anything about them in the telling of my story, I am not angry. I have forgiven my parents. They didn't know what they didn't know. They were a product of their environments and of their DNA. I forgave them because they were a product of mental, physical and emotional abuse by their parents. My father was a product of an affair. Back then, you just didn't do that or get caught. On numerous occasions, his mother would beat him and was very cruel to him. I found out when I was older, that his mother beat him horribly bad one time and left him for dead.

Thankfully, his father took him to the hospital, and he recovered. However, I can't even imagine what an awful and lasting impact that beating had on my father. My mother was the third of four children. Despite having four children, my Grandmother really did not like children. On two occasions, she abandoned her children. I was with my mother, when she was dying. My mom was dying and was practically unresponsive. As I was sitting there with her, she suddenly started to cry and yelled for her mother to stop. Then she looked straight into my eyes and said, "She (her mother) just kept walking away from her with her suitcase, got on the bus and never looked back." I couldn't hold my tears back. I know that my parents were adults, but they were also broken. Just like so many of us, they didn't have the tools they needed to heal. They did not have support and counseling, like we have now. In addition to realizing that my parents were wounded and lacked access to the resources they needed to heal, I didn't just forgive them for them, I forgave them for me.

There is no reason for me to carry their burdens.

Hanson Childhood Memories

When my family finally settled down, my dad was a superintendent for Dobson Brothers Construction Company. We traveled a lot, so I attended several different schools in one year. As a result, I was able to make friends quite easily. When my brothers started to go to junior high school, my parents thought it was best not to travel and change schools so much. Therefore, they bought a house in Lincoln, Nebraska. After that, we were raised with a paintbrush and a drywall knife in our hand. My dad did a lot of the construction himself and my mom was a painter, wall-paperer and decorator. We were raised with construction minds. My brothers ended up being framers, roofers and drywallers and I became a painter, drywaller, wall paperer and interior designer. At around the age of nine, I enrolled in a program called the *White Gloves and Party Manner.* The program taught young girls the etiquette of silverware and plate placement, how to walk, sit, talk, dress and many other important graces that aren't taught very much anymore. At the end of that program, we modeled clothes for Hovland-Swanson, an iconic department store in Nebraska. This was the highlight of the program. Not long after that, I ended up with the Hong-Kong flu which a lot of people at that time, especially children, died from. I remember that it was pretty serious. I especially recall the time my parents took me to the doctor, because they were not sure whether I was going to live. Thankfully, however, I survived.

My mom was an entrepreneur, who was always offering painting classes. She was either teaching classes on ceramics or porcelain dolls. Sometimes, she even taught people about raising puppies because we had a Cocker Spaniel. Therefore, she was also raising puppies in order to make money from selling them. She was the entrepreneur of the family. My dad typically worked a 9 to 5 day. He was very good at teaching us the importance of having a strong work ethic. During that period, my parents seemed to fight a lot about money. My dad was a severe alcoholic. We learned at a very young age to wear a facade and to pretend that everything was okay. However, we knew that things were not okay. They were very physically abusive.

Unfortunately, my mom was as mentally, emotionally and physically abusive, as my dad was verbally and physically abusive to us kids. We eventually moved out into the country, where they built a large dog kennel facility, where we raised German Shepherds, Siberian Huskies, Cocker Spaniels and Lhasa Apsos. We also boarded dogs at this facility. We were very successful with the dog business. We also showed the dogs in shows and won several awards for the dogs we bred. Despite this business success, as time went on, the fighting, arguing, screaming and yelling grew to be very intense. Therefore, my brothers and I found ways to occupy our time. We learned ways to divert that negativity into positivity. I would sew my Barbie clothes on an old sewing machine. It was given to me by an old woman that we stayed with, when we were on the road. Her name was Mrs. Stuchenschmidt. She was a stern old woman. However, she took a liking to me and when we left, she gave me her sewing machine. I think she just wanted a new one and giving me the old machine was her way of justifying her need for a new machine. I was about nine years old then and I was also sewing my mom's

STEPHANIE FORD

dresses at that time. When my father would come home, I would unpack his suitcase, wash and dry his laundry, and then reload his suit-cases, for him to go back on the road. The fighting and abuse were starting to intensify in my home. I know it was because of the drinking and all of the pressures of everyday life. Life was just hard, and it was weighing on my parents.

Madness at Mount Rushmore

I remember going on a vacation in the Black Hills, Rapid City, South Dakota and Mount Rushmore. My little brother, Patrick, and my Uncle Gary and his family; Aunt Carolyn, Gary Jr., and Tara Dee (Jason hadn't been born yet) were with us. It was 1972. It had started to rain. We all were down in the Mount Rushmore cave. They called us all back, because a big boulder had crashed through the ceiling. We all came back up and got into our car. We started driving up the mountains and watched the water con-tinue to rise. It was scary and unforgettable. We even saw horses floating by us! Finally, we were lucky enough to get to our hotel. It was an A-

Frame style building. We had to cross a little creek to get to the other side, where the restaurant was. It was still raining. We went across the little bridge back to our hotel. The rain then really started coming down heavy. I vividly recall that there was a dog barking in the back of the hotel. Suddenly, there was a tremendous mountain slide, and then no more barking dog. We all ran to the edge of the A-frame part of the hotel. We were on the second floor. The owner called us all into the A-frame, where he and his family lived. It was just in time because not long after he called us in, the part of the building, where we were all standing just before that, cracked and separated! We all would have fallen into the rising water. As the waters kept rising, we stayed there. However, panic was definitely setting in. We saw people floating by us on mattresses and in trailers. The screams of the people rose and fell like the raging water. In the middle of the storm, the gas station across the street was being looted. The owner went to his closet, got out his gun and started shooting at them. The mountains were sliding all around us. By morning, the National Guard had arrived with gigantic looking dump trucks, which they used to evacuate as many people as possible. They placed a large plank with a cable attached across the raging creek and started carrying us across the creek and putting us in the truck. That when my aunt started screaming, "Where is Tara? Where is Tara!" The entire time that she screamed for Tara, my aunt had Tara clinched in her arms and didn't even realize it. We were all in shock. I don't remember how many people they were able to put in the trucks, but I remember how kind the guards were. They just kept reassuring us that now we were going to be okay. They took us up to the Mount Rushmore Visitor's Center and made shift shelters. I just remember hearing all of the crying and the many touching stories of loved ones, who had been lost in the slides. We ended up staying there for a couple of days, until my Dad's boss drove up to get us. We lost all of our belongings, but we were all safe and that's what truly mattered.

I can't even describe the amount of damage and destruction that we saw as we drove back home, Although I was a young child, I will never forget the miracle of my entire family escaping that devastation.

Fits of Rage, Glimmers of Hope

Shortly after our awful Mount Rushmore saga, my second to oldest brother started drinking and smoking. He also introduced me to smoking and I started to smoke cigarettes when I was just twelve years old. He wasn't interested in getting me to smoke. He just wanted me to smoke, so that I would not tell on him. I remember at a very early age driving him around in the country in an Opel Kadett, because he kept getting too drunk to drive.

Despite the grown-up issues that I dealt with in my childhood, during our time in Waverly, Nebraska, I had also some great childhood experiences. I was a majorette for our school and also a pom-pom girl. I was so proud of myself. My parents only came once to see me perform and that was at the State Fair.

The fighting only escalated with my parents. During one of their many fits of rage, my dad picked up a chair to hit my mom. She grabbed me and put me in front of her, so that he would not continue. Needless to say, that was an extremely traumatic experience for me. The fighting and arguing between the two of them was traumatic enough for me as a young girl. However, for my mother to grab me to shield herself from harm, is an incident that stuck with me for years.

After that particular fight, things started to get even crazier. One night my oldest brother, Rob, came home five minutes late. I was sitting at the top of the stairs. I watched my dad tell Rob to put his hands down to his side and take it like a man, He then punched my brother in the mouth. He had braces at the time and the blow to his mouth broke one of the braces' wires. The wire pushed right through my brother's bottom lip. It didn't matter. He hit him again! I sat at the top of the stairs crying uncontrollably. I didn't know what to do. I know that my parents were fighting, and things were escalating. They both ended up having affairs. I remember a Thanksgiving when my mom went to California with her boyfriend, while my dad had a Thanksgiving dinner for us. However, he was having affairs too. We knew about them because they'd also fight about the cheating.

While we were still out in the countryside, I knew that I had a spiritual need, so I went to catechisms every Wednesday night. I went to youth group meetings every Saturday night, and I went to church on Sundays. Even if my parents did not go to church, I went just so that I could stay from them. Besides, I needed God in my life.

When we moved back into the city, my mom told me that she and my dad were getting a divorce. As soon as my mom told me about it, I started to cry. She said that if she had known that I would not be "adult enough" to handle the news of the divorce, that she would not have told me the way she did. I was only 13 at the time. Even though they fought like crazy and even with all their flaws, I still loved them.

After the divorce, my mom went to work full-time. As a result, my youngest brother and I were left to fend for ourselves most of the time. We cleaned the house and cooked. My oldest two brothers had gone into the service. They joined the Marines, so we didn't see them much.

Not much time passed, before my stepdad came into the picture. He was an amazing man -- a true cowboy-- and one of the most honest men I had ever met.

Trouble Keeps on Finding Me

When I was 13 years old, I met our neighbors. One of our neighbors was an older man, who was getting a divorce from his wife. I recall us having major parties at his house all the time. I was introduced to speed and many other mind-altering drugs. It was around that time in my life, when I started smoking pot and drinking alcohol. As a matter of fact, I used to sneak out of the basement window, when my mom and dad went to sleep. I'd leave our home and go party with all the older people at that house. One time, we were out partying and noticed the police coming down the alley. I jumped under a car, so that I would not be seen with their spotlights. Another time I jumped in between a breezeway and hid behind stacks of wood. The cops shone their spotlight right over the top of my head but miraculously, I never got caught. Those were crazy times.

One night, while hanging out with the older crowd next door on my fourteenth birthday, one of the men there decided to give me a birthday present that I'd never be able to forget. He raped me. He was twenty-six years old. When his wife found out, she divorced him. From that time on, my life took a downward spiral. As you can imagine, the drugs and all of the partying got out of hand. I was glad that my stepdad, Charles Yonker, had come into my mom's life. This is because once he did, things seemed to level out a little bit. On my sixteenth birthday, he bought me a 1962 Chevy Impala. I loved that car, but I especially loved the stability that he brought to our lives.

That stability was unfortunately short-lived. Somehow, my biological father was able to get custody of me. I am not sure how he got custody of me, and not of my little brother, but you know how crazy the court system can be. Anyway, I ended up going to live with my father in his apartment. Not too long before I was sent

STEPHANIE FORD

to live with him, he had come to my mother's home. The two of them got into a huge fight, which ended up with my mom being knocked to the floor. After he threw her onto the floor, he kicked her in the ribs, grabbed the phone cord and wrapped the wire around her neck. While he almost choked her to death, my brother grabbed him from behind to get him off of her. Shortly after my brother was able to separate the two of them, the police showed up. Things were just as crazy when I moved in with him. I think we were all doing drugs and partying a lot to escape our reality. While I lived with my biological father, I went to school and tried to do things like a normal young girl would. However, day-to-day living with him was just not normal. He was a severe alcoholic.

One night he came home after work and found that I had not rinsed the dishes off, before I had put them into the dishwasher. We got into a heated argument and he ended up throwing me over the door of the dishwasher. I landed on my tailbone, broke it and hit my head on the door casing by the floor. It pretty much knocked me out, but that did not stop his attack on me.

He picked me up and started beating me up against the wall and then threw me into my room. That was my last straw. At that point in my life, I decided that I was not going to stay there anymore. I'd had had enough of the abuse.

I was dating a guy who had just gotten out of the Marines. He was a drug dealer. We needed to carry guns with us. During one of his illegal dealings, my boyfriend did one of his clients wrong. This client was determined to get his money back, one way or another. The people we associated ourselves with then, were all scandalous people. I was coming home late from a party one night, when I heard someone following me. As I walked to my apartment, I heard footsteps behind me getting louder, so I reached into my purse and pulled out my 22 pistols. When I turned around, ready to pull the trigger, I saw that the man following me was the guy that my boyfriend had done wrong. Thankfully, he saw my gun and backed off. When I told my boyfriend what had happened, they found him beat him up and left him for dead. These are the types of people I associated with at that time in my life. Thankfully, I knew that I needed to make a change. I knew the course that I was taking was not a good one, so I decided that I was going to leave. Remember, I was still in high school. I was trying to go to school, party and work a couple of different jobs all at once. I called my brother. He came and got me and took me to the small town where he lived.

Desperate to Begin Again

My biological dad didn't know where I had gone. He called my mom and she just said that she knew I had been missing for two weeks. Since I was living in the same town as my brother, I went to the school there and registered to finish my senior year. Finally, I had a fresh start -- for what seemed like a millisecond. Sadly, the freshness wore off quickly and trouble found me again. I had not been there long, before my brother was busted for 4.8 pounds of pot which was followed by a horrific tragedy, in which I lost my dear friend in a terrible car accident.

We were in a 1965 Chevelle doing at least 125 miles per hour around a freshly armor coated road. The driver lived on the road but didn't realize that it had been repaved that day. We lost control of the car. It flipped end over end and sideways five times, then hit an electrical pole. The wire from the pole wrapped around the car and we landed thirty-seven feet away in a cornfield. The driver was thrown out of the car and the car rolled on top of him. It flung him another thirty-five feet. I managed to pull my hair out of the interior light. It was wrapped around the light several times. I had hair down to the bottom of my back then. I managed to crawl out of the window that the power line pole had crossed. I got the door open enough to pull my girlfriend out from under the dashboard. We all had serious cuts and lacerations. There was blood everywhere. Upon realizing what we had just endured, my friend went into shock. I got on top of her to cover her and keep her warm, while our other friend ran to the nearest farmhouse to get help. My other dear friend who was with us was named Donny. Donny died.

After the accident, we went to the scene to see exactly where the car was and to see what we had lived through. The principal of my school was there. He told me that I needed to be in school and I actually got a detention! The principal at the high school did not like me because I came from a large school. He and his staff did everything they could to discourage me from coming into the school. As a matter of fact, one time he put his hand across the door to block me from entering. When the tardy bell rang, he told me to get a tardy slip. I ended up with seven different offenses for stupid stuff. One day I just got fed up. I took all of the detentions into the principal's office and told him to stick them up his ass, then I walked out. I had just had enough. My stepdad came to my home and said I was going to go to school. He grabbed my arm and started pushing me to go to school. I threw my books at him and said, "I am!" He backhand slapped me and split my lip open. I yelled, "You are not my dad! You had no right to hit me!" With a very sad and very quiet look, he stared me in my eyes and said in a very low, soft voice, "I wash my hands of you."

It was not the reaction that I was looking for. As a matter of fact, his words cut me to the heart. He was the only one who truly had my best interests at heart. My mom came flying down the road in the car, because she just knew that my stepdad was very upset. He got in his pickup truck and drove away. I got in the car with my mom and we drove around.

I decided to quit school.

A few months later, my brother had to appear in court. While I was sitting in court with him (he was facing prison time), I looked at the attorneys, the judge and my brother. I thought to myself, "What the hell am I doing with my life?" Here I am, a senior in high school, and I'm sitting in a courtroom with my brother who came to help me get more stability in my life. However, he is now facing time in prison for selling drugs.

At that moment in my life, I decided I needed to finish high school. I went to the counselor to see what I needed to do to graduate with my class. And I did it! My stepdad was very proud of me and he told me so. He was my rock. I looked up to him so much because, although he never told me he loved me, he never had to. I always felt his pure love for me. I knew he loved me because of the way he treated me and talked to me. Everything that he did for me was in my best interest. I truly did love him.

On Closure & Moving Forward

Sometimes people do not get the opportunity to go back and get closure from the things that happened in their lives. However, that was not the case for me. I was offered a paint job in a small town called Loup City. I wasn't there for very long, but I had a lot of history in that city. It was where I was in a car accident that killed the driver. It was where I'd gotten married and almost died giving birth to my baby girl. Loup City was where I stopped going to school. It was also where many people didn't want me, because I was from a big city and I was a drug dealer. Who wants a known drug dealer to be in your town? Anyway, I went to Loup City and I did the job. As I was driving into this small town, I started feeling very anxious. I wasn't a very nice person when I was there. When I was last there, I was just doing what I needed to do to survive. I wasn't going to let the memories take over my life. I had the opportunity to go and do my job. I stripped wallpaper, skim coated walls and painted.

In addition to working, while in Loup City, I met with my best friend at that time. I'd named my first-born daughter after her. She was also the Maid of Honor at my wedding. We reconnected and had an amazing conversation. We just picked right up, where we left off. I also had the chance to get some unresolved issues addressed. I was kind of angry with the town, because of how they treated me while I was there. However, I was older and was able to understand why some of those things happened. I was able to get some closure regarding that part of my life. I embraced the fact that I was there for a season and was even able to forgive myself for being the person I was at that time. I am definitely no longer that person. However, living through that experience molded me and ultimately made me a better person.

Although I haven't accomplished everything that is in my heart to do yet, I have come much farther than I was in life. I am now not only a student of personal and professional development I am a trainer. I led a national personal and professional development morning conference call. It's a 15-minute jump start your day kind of call and professionals call from across the nation to be inspired. I clearly got my serial entrepreneurial spirit from parents. This is because in addition to authoring my memoirs, training and speaking, I own and operate both a cleaning and faux painting business.

I am excited to share that you'll be able to read my complete memoir, when it's released in the New Year (It's impossible for me to tell you the entire, miraculous story now). However, what I hope you believe from reading this part of my story is that,

Your life is valuable no matter what you have been through.

I also want you to rest assured that God will never leave you alone. If you do not quit on yourself; there is always hope for you! You are a strong woman.

I took care of so many people and their children, that I forgot to take care of myself. It is very important that you take care of yourself while you are caring for others, so you don't find yourself isolated, limited and too exhausted to give anything more.

I am a living testament to what God's grace, strength and favor can do for you. I am here to help women like you to know and perhaps to remember that you can be empowered and can overcome your past, no matter what! Whether you have survived drug addiction, rape, abuse, divorce or some other hardship, the pain that was inflicted on you does not have to define you. You do not have to let pain and unforgiveness win.

It all starts with YOU making a decision for YOUR life.

You have to finally get fed up enough that *you* make the changes that *you* need and want to make.

You only need to hope and to find a loving community to teach you the things you need to learn to sharpen your professional and personal skills, so that you can gain the coping and over-coming strategies that you need in order to deal with your life's disappointments. When you do this, you will move on to claim and share your greatness.

LESSONS IN THE VALLEY

Elyce Taylor

Chapter 6

Yes, Ms. Taylor, our system is showing that your vehicle was recovered this morning. You didn't know? the GM representative said. She sounded surprised. "No!" I angrily replied, "I was IN MY CAR THIS morning! I had no idea that my car was repossessed.

I was pissed, when I walked outside, and I couldn't locate my new Malibu. I was in the process of picking up the wet clothes that I had dropped while doing laundry, when I realized that my car was missing. I thought the car was stolen. I did not learn that it had been recovered, until I checked the locate my Chevrolet owner app on my phone. When I tracked my vehicle, the app showed that the car was parked in one of my city's well- known auto pound yards.

I laughed. Laughed? You're probably asking, "What the hell could she possibly laugh about?" When I realized what really happened to me that morning, I had an out of body experience. My mind left, when I was standing in my home, and for a split second I was thrust approximately eight months into the future. I saw myself standing in the most gorgeous $1295 C. Louboutin spiked stilettos. (I'd eventually planned to purchase these for myself). In my vision, I was swinging my freshly oiled legs into my new Maserati. This vision of my days to come lasted all of 30 seconds, before I snapped back to reality. When I did, the reality I face caused me to totally lose it. I was exceptionally angry and frustrated, because I'd called General Motors Finance that morning, to tell them that I would be mailing them the $635.00 past due balance noted in the email they had sent to me the previous week. Interestingly, I received that email from them that very same day. It was one week from the day they'd taken my car. The re-possession of my vehicle could not have happened at a worse time!

My cousin, Markesha, was murdered the week before. I was dropping my clothes at the cleaners on my way to the grocery store and had to cook for the repast. Markesha was a beautiful soul. She had just gotten married a little over a year ago. She and Isaac, her husband, who she had been with for over eight years, loved and parented five little boys, all under the age of nine. Markesha was an excellent mother.

Isaac and Markesha had a recurring issue with the mother (Alicia) of her younger brother's children. Tragically, things festered into a volatile situation during the custody battle between her brother and Alicia. The situation became so violent, that it ended with the murder of my cousin at the hands of Alicia's girlfriend. She stabbed Markesha in the parking lot of a bank in Peoria. I share the link to the news report at the end of this chapter.

The craziest thing about all of this, is that my cousin was murdered by someone who involved herself in a situation that had nothing to do with her. The case is still open and pending at this time.

Losing Markesha the way I did, hurt me very deeply. I only disclosed to a few people that I had the chance to see Markesha the week before she was murdered. She was no more than ten minutes away from me on Thanksgiving Day. However, instead of going to see her, I waved a visit to that side of my family, to hang out with the cousins who I was just getting close to on my father's side of the family. I'll never forget saying, "I'll catch them next time." However, the next time I saw my cousin, Markesha, was at her viewing. She wore all white, was lying in a beautiful white casket with pink embroidery, surrounded by delicate flowers that were the same color as her wedding colors -- fuchsia and turquoise.

I literally dragged my closest cousin, William, back inside of the funeral home, walked past everyone, including Isaac because I didn't know yet what to say to him, and into the viewing room. As I stood behind two other really sad people who had come to pay their respects, I could see her hands. The next things I knew, William and his mom, Floreine, had to carry me into another room. I had my first anxiety attack in almost a year.

It took me a few minutes to pull myself together. However, with the help of my cousins, who literally held me up and did breathing exercises with me, I was able to walk back into the room. I spent the next few minutes staring at her made-up face and flawlessly curled hair which had been done by her mom, Nicole. I noticed that my cousin's hands were swollen but manicured. I stared at her hands, until my mind began to play tricks on me. "She just moved, I imagined. "I think I saw a slight movement." I said to myself hoping that somehow the lifeless body of my dear cousin, mother to five young, heart-broken boys, might miraculously regain consciousness. That could happen, I mused. After all, Markesha was just too strong to die from a stab wound. I don't care where the knife landed!

My mind drifted back to my own story. I was in a situation that was very similar to Markesha's. In my case, the woman was my little brother's ex-girlfriend. I actually remember telling Markesha about how I dealt with that difficult part of my life.

Keep Going

How many times in your life have you regretted a thought? A word? An action? Better yet, how many times did you not think, not speak or not act? If I had a dollar for every time, I regretted NOT opening my mouth, I wouldn't be working so hard. I'd already be a millionaire. So, what now? What do we do with our regrets now?

Let it Go

We expend so much energy focusing on our past, that we forget to breathe in the blessings of the new day. We minimize the new chance that we get to put our best foot forward. The only thing that we can do with regret is accept the lesson, learn from it, make better decisions moving forward and use the energy and drive we get from wanting to do better, to design ourselves an amazing future.

OVERstand that EVERYTHING in life happens for a reason. This is even if you don't understand at the time. I had a near-fatal accident three days before my thirtieth birthday. I thought it was the worst thing that ever happened to me, when in hindsight, it turned out to be one of the best!

First, I tell you that my first reaction was to laugh when my car was repossessed and now, I am telling you that a near-fatal accident turned out to be one of the best things that ever happened to me. Let me explain. I will start by admitting that, I was a dumbass. Do you want to talk about times of great regret? I have regret, because I should have waited to turn left. I sat waiting at a stale green light and was t-boned by a lovely Mercedes SUV. I didn't regret the choice to turn that day, because I checked for oncoming traffic and thought I had plenty of time to make that turn. Obviously, my RAV-4 disagreed.

Unlike the proverbial moment right before the impact of a crash like the one I was in; I did not have a was not my life flashing before my eyes. It was more of a "Oh SHIT, this is about to be so bad" moment. I remember closing my eyes to minimize the likelihood of glass getting in them. My truck was totaled. The damage was irreparable, and I'd only had my car a little over six months.

I remember opening my eyes and seeing all my airbags deployed. Everything that I had in the car was all over the front seat, including the dozen donuts that I had planned to take to work that day. They were strewn all over the place. My nose was burning and there was a strong unfamiliar stench. Something was definitely burning. I was in pain. I'd sustained a busted lip, a dislocated right shoulder, chemical burns from the Takata airbag materials and a left wrist that needed to spend the next few weeks in a cast. Screw all of the pain. The hissing sound I heard was so loud, that I just knew my truck was about to explode. It never exploded (or caught on fire for that matter). However, I panicked and screamed for the people walking around my car who were not sure what to do. I wanted them to help me get out. I didn't know if they could hear me outside of the imaginary flames that I swore were about to surround my vehicle. Therefore, I took my injured wrist high enough for my fingers to grip the door handle, kicked it open and slid my ass out of that truck in record time.

I made it approximately a yard, before I fell to the ground. This was where I received helped from a very attractive nurses' aide, until the ambulance arrived a few minutes later. I remembered one of the EMTs from helping me a few months back, when I passed out at work (reason still unknown).His job was to convince me to go to the hospital. The thought of that ambulance ride bill, kept me apprehensive and trying to convince him that I would be fine.

I was told that I needed to miss work for six weeks to recover. However, against my mother's valid arguments for me to take time to heal and to make my job grow more appreciative of me in my absence, I went back to work after a week and a half. I'd come out of the sling and had one arm for use.

Why did I *really* go back so soon?

The simple answer at that time was, these bills! I knew that I should be eligible for medical time off, but I wasn't sure at what cost. Just the thought of the medical bills was overwhelming. After a conversation with our manager, I also realized that I would be leaving, Jessica, my supervisor, hanging for weeks by herself. I'd stopped by the dealer on my way back home from the hospital follow-up (a week after the accident) to let my manager Bill know what the physician recommended regarding my time off. Bill's response was, "Well, I know what the doctor is telling you but you're a big girl. You know your limits. We'd like you to come back sooner, if you can."

Are you laughing at me yet? I am, because I doubt that he would have said this to Jessica, but I digress. I ended up leaving that dealership a year later for three reasons. First, the salary was too low. I was earning less than $40K a year and the raise, I almost died to get, never happened. Second, the politics became too much to deal with. I was offered a position as the fifth service writer. Despite the additional training I had begun, I was not promoted. Instead, they hired another white man two weeks after I left. Third, there was no room for me to grow there. I'd clearly outgrown what I had been doing and there was no other position for me to move into at that company. It was time to go.

Growth

How many times have you been in a situation, where you looked back and wondered: "Why did I accept that?!" It's time to forgive yourself and not do it again. I'm talking about accepting less than you deserve at work, in relationships and in life in general. DON'T DO IT AGAIN. You deserve more.

I spent much of my life being a yes-woman, who accepted peanuts when I should've gotten steak. A great deal of that stemmed from my personal lack of self-esteem and self-confidence. The question is, "Are you ready to share your truth with the world, despite how it makes others feel?" No. However, my mentor, Jéneen, made it abundantly clear that growth will not happen in your comfort zone. You have to leave it. Write this on your vision wall:

"You have to do what others are not willing to do, to get to where others will not go."

I am a vastly different person than I was a decade ago. Thank God for adversity. Had I not been through some extremely challenging times, I would not have grown nearly as much as I have since February 2019. Growing up (and I'm told this is indeed an Aquarius thing), I was fiercely insecure. I mean my self-esteem was LOW.

Parents often don't realize how much power the things they say and do have on developing their children's mindset. Our parents' decisions and behaviors play a very large role in the decisions we make as adults. Ladies, you are the first role model to your girls. Gentlemen, you are the first man your daughters will love. How you treat them, and how they see you treat their mothers, will play a huge role in how they accept treatment from potential suitors. Ladies, you show your sons how to treat a woman and how to be receive love. Gentlemen, you show your sons how to give love, what treatment to accept, chivalry, and how to accept strengths and weaknesses.

I was deeply impacted by things my parents may have thought were insignificant. My mom said and did some things when I was younger that I wish had been a bit more encouraging. However, I *OVER*stand every sacrifice she made for me. Even if it wasn't the best idea, and to show my appreciation for her, Finis is getting the first house that I purchase when I earn my first million dollars in the markets! My dad (unintentionally) made me feel the brunt of the resentment he harbored towards my mom. Understand that when my daddy does something for me, it's nice! I'd go over to his home every other weekend and RELAX. I'd sleep in and he'd cook whatever my little sister and I wanted for breakfast. The place was always clean and the tomboy — me -- had access to video games galore. All of this was in stark contrast to my mother's house which, until I was in high school, was a volatile environment filled with domestic violence between her and my stepdad. With that and the fact that I was the oldest of four siblings, I had a lot of responsibility. So again, I'd go to Daddy's and relax. Still, there were times when I'd bear the weight of much of the negativity that my dad felt. After years of counseling, I finally realized that it had a significant impact on me. One time, an hour-long scolding from my dad began with his disappointment in a bad choice I made and ended with him saying, "I have the worst two baby mamas in the world!"

That last statement was one with which I totally disagreed. This is because, even at my young age (and maybe because I loved them both so much), I unfortunately, had the "pleasure" of dealing with three situations of baby mama drama for too many years in a row. I'm talking about fights, vandalism, threats, harassment, jail time, murder hits, arson and No Stalking orders that were issued through the courts. I'll delve more into those details another time.

Nonetheless, everything I endured helped my growth. Everything I endured made me a strong woman. For one thing, had I known in high school that I was a strong as I am, I would've never allowed a girl to bully me. I would have never allowed people, and their jokes, to make me feel less valuable than I am. I laughed to keep from crying, but it hurt. It's funny; I often wonder how much further I would be in life, if I had the confidence that I do now. Those thoughts can either propel you or hinder you, so be careful how much time you spend on regret and on wondering what-if.

Why?

There are two types of stress: distress and eu-stress. Eustress is simply, motivation. It keeps you going. It only applies the pressure necessary or beneficial to accomplishing a task. The antag-onist of eustress is distress. Scientific reports have shown that stress correlates with a decline in health. Distress impacts your immune system and makes you more vulnerable and susceptible to illnesses. Therefore, what's the source of your stress? Financial woes? Relationships? Family? Health ailments? Some underlying cause?

In retrospect, last year was the worst financial year I had. It was due, in part, to a lack of clarity. There are many people who behave as if the world owes us something. It doesn't. What you want is out there for you. You just have to go get it. You have to create your own economy.

In the era of the Trump administration (whether you support him or not), it's clear that the economic environment has changed. Where, here in the CORPORATION of The United States (look it up), the middle class is dissipating. Many of us, primarily those who live UNDER the recognized poverty line, feel the downside of these changes. We've got to create our own economy. President Trump has changed tax laws so much, that it is abundantly clear that the laws benefit those who are business owners; not W-2 employees or the 1099 self-employed, but business OWNERS.

I've known this for quite some time and have launched multiple home-based businesses. I did well in a few (up to an extra $1000 a week, at one point) and poorly in most. I've always been a hustler, going back to my days of cutting dope during my time in college (it was like one time as a favor) to grinding the way I do now. Yet, my bank account is still missing some zeroes. I know it's coming, because I work, I affirm, and I align myself in preparation for it to come. Most millionaires see the mansion, the cars, the money and the lifestyle in their minds, before it becomes tangible. We must do the same. We know that faith without work is dead and it's simple, we put in the work.

2017 and 2018 were years filled with heartache, health ailments and financial loss. However, I remembered and held onto my "WHY". There were multiple times in my adult life, where I endured possible and actual eviction, vehicle recovery, volatile relationships and major financial loss. However, each of these situations brought me to a place of clarity and major breakthrough.

In 2018, I broke up with my boyfriend, when I found out that he'd gotten someone else pregnant. I got back with the man who had broken my heart eight years earlier. My son's dad came into my life during the time between the break-up and reuniting with my former heartbreak. As you can see; I wasn't making great choices. However, I've seen much worse. Each one of these men told me they'd become better men because of me. However, from where I stood, I wasn't doing so great. I questioned for months, why I was sent on yet another roller-coaster with my ex, when my son and I were okay. Then I gained clarity.

I NEEDED this second time with him. It was not for long term but because of the way things were supposed to happen. He is the only person in the world who I could lean on and would have completely trusted to get me away from my job. I hold no regrets. In that time, I was able to focus more on becoming the Master Foreign Exchange Market trader I want to be. He carried things for a bit, and it felt good to have a provider around who filled me with joy on our good days.

The break-up came after I prayed and prayed for clarity. The Most- High set it in my lap on Mother's Day 2018, so there would be no denying what I found. He was cheating but the strength I showed after I learned the truth, was worth every bit of the roller coaster ride on which he had me. You could tell how much I'd grown, because I decided that the situation wasn't worth the ugly in me. Eight years earlier, was a different story. This is where I had to check the statute of limitations laws in Illinois and Indiana. I'm good. So, here's the interesting part. I shot his truck up eight years before. I mean I emptied two full clips from my .380 into every recess of his semi- truck that I could. The situation, after everything I went through, called for it. At least, I thought so at the time.

I remember skating around the icy lot, where his and his dad's truck sat parked in East Chicago, Indiana, at between one and two in the morning. My little sister, who had recently been through her own ordeal, sat in my parked Ford Escape with the engine running. I don't know why she came with me, but I was glad she did. I was glad she came, until one of the bullets I shot ricocheted into my truck and landed on my dashboard less than a foot away from her. Her scream among the hissing tires and bullet echoes in the freezing, silent night, was the only thing that snapped me out of my crazed anger. I was in a 'destroy and conquer' zone! It's crazy when I think back to that night. The police never came. What's even better? HE never came.

Fast forward to this break-up. I told him not to use the key I had given him. I'd broken up with him, when my bills were due. Even worse, I no longer had any savings. Now what? At this point, I was jobless and had no income. The emotional stress I endured for a month (yeah, my bounce back game was strong this time) after that break-up, caused me to lose everything I had put into trading in the market. I was a novice trader. You should *never* trade, when emotional. You also should never rush the skillset. I did both and I took a rather large hit because of it.

Be Humble. Remain Humble

Around that time in my life, is when I looked into Rideshare, Uber and Lyft. I still had a son to feed and provide a roof for, so I started driving.

Rideshare is a very humbling experience. I was doing rather well and averaging $1100 a week at first. Then things changed. A host of factors caused the dramatic turn that my bank account experienced. These included the weather, saturation in the driver market and mistakes that I made in my driving strategy. Remember this rule of thumb, if it isn't broke, don't fix it. My mistakes cost me a great deal of income.

I've been driving for the past six months. I will personally say that, with over 2000 rides under my belt, I've been reminded that most of the world is good. My thoughts were the exact opposite for years. I lost many friends, due to gun violence and other forms of murder. I came home from undergrad at Tuskegee University, got my Master's in Business Administration and was left with over $200,000 in student loan debt and a job that wouldn't cover that debt. This is the definition of irony! We go to school, sign for all these loans and get a job to pay the loans we get from school. Here I am, part of the 65% displaced. I among those who don't work in their chosen field. Therefore, as far as I was concerned, there were no jobs in Chicago. I mean I did it the right way, right? Yet, I was still struggling. Have you been there?

Check on your rideshare driving friends. It gets interesting out here! Imagine – if you will- you drive and heighten the collision risk. You pick up total strangers and you go to unfamiliar areas. Fun Fact: The average person meets a murderer at least 10 times in their life. So, I can only imagine how many I've had in my car! Child molesters. Rapists. I wonder how many times someone considered an attempt to kidnap me or worse. Did I pick someone up, after they committed a heinous crime? You never know. What I do know, is that I've had to check two passengers for sexual harassment. I actually put one out on the side of the expressway and received a threat from Lyft for deactivation for doing so. However, my heart wouldn't have broken, had he accidentally been hit by oncoming traffic. I tell everyone to be aware of what their gut tells you. If something doesn't feel right about your passenger's vibe, then do not let them in your car. You never know.

Despite the fear factor, I lean more positively on the fact that I have met some phenomenal people who either needed to take a ride with ME or I needed to meet them. Many of my passengers have been unforgettable. I've gotten job offers, date requests, stock tips, gifts, even my first speaking engagement! My first day included a hand massage from a massage therapist, and 45 minutes of singing from two pool riders, who started out as strangers and continued contact long after our ride. I went to one of their performances a few months later and sat with the other.

There IS an abundance of money out here. You must find and utilize the best vehicle to reach it! However, if your *WHY* isn't big enough, you WILL miss out on opportunities, you WILL look back with regret, your decisions will be based on how you feel in the moment versus how you felt when you made 'the' decision and you WILL make excuses. It will all keep you from reaching your potential.

Let me go back, because I'm writing under the assumption that everyone reading this collection knows exactly what a *WHY* is. In clarification, your *WHY* -is simply your *reason.* This is the reason you chose to take on the opportunity, accept that position and deal with the stress which comes with them. Your *WHY* will have you up in the wee hours of the morning to practice and study something, that while it may stretch you in the moment, will bless you in the long-term. Your WHY will make you get up every day and go to a job you despise going to, to work with people you despise working with, in a place you despise. Your WHY will make you understand the importance of short-term sacrifice for long-term benefits. Your WHY will keep you grounded and remind you, although you may have reached that goal, you cannot stop there.

Your WHY is strong enough to make you cry. It is not necessarily in pain, fear or loss. However, it is in realization of the blessing for which you have worked so hard.

My why is the legacy I plan to leave my grandchildren's children. After a recent conversation with one of the smartest individuals I ever met about my five-year plan (I hope you have one written down by the way), I realized that my plan had to go much deeper, than the surface I was on.

My business partners and I have discussed many times that upon trading mastery, we would go out and save the masses! How? Why? Chicago is like a 'Tale of Two Cities,' because you have the beautiful (probably gentrified) affluent, tourist areas and then you have the low-income "violence ridden" areas. Our goals are to reach back to teach others, especially those in low income areas, the skillset of trading currency on the foreign exchange market. Doing this could change the dynamic of these areas. Although money has been deemed the root of all evil, I have also seen it forge some unconventional partnerships.

What many people don't understand is that we (African Americans, Black people, Moorish Americans, the Asiatic Black Man, whatever your favorite term is) have forgotten the beauty in our bones. There are people out here, who believe that Black History started with slavery. Let me remind you that slavery was nothing more than an interruption of our greatness. They didn't kidnap slaves. They kidnapped doctors, teachers, inventors, entrepreneurs, traders, lawyers, etc. We have had negativity beaten into our brains so long, that it now comes out in our thoughts, speech, actions and even our efforts.

Africans created and achieved amazing heights, long before the 20th and 21st century technologies. Look at the Obelisk of Axum. It "resembles" the Washington Monument, which was constructed with the huge machines and technologies of today. By contrast, the Obelisk was erected centuries before! While many of us are aware of these amazing things, you have people out here who think that Africa is nothing more than huts and the poor. Uganda looks like Chicago! I say that all of our ancestors (whether in Africa or elsewhere) did great things and we've forgotten many of our abilities.

In teaching people a skillset, which they have believed for years was "only for the wealthy people (predominantly white people), we have to remember we hold just as much claim, we can take it to new heights and we can literally save many people around us. We hold the keys, but we must be led back to the right doors.

Decide

Everything begins with a decision, even our mistakes. We've all been in this place, whether you've run into a brick wall deciding on an outfit, a decision that would affect the longevity of a company, or a decision to give someone another opportunity. Some people make their best decisions, when they're backed against a wall and under pressure. Others decide best, with proper planning.

What many have failed to realize and what some found out later, is that each decision causes a ripple effect. Just like a pebble thrown into water causes ripples that expand out into the vast body of water into which it is thrown; decisions affect us and those around us in many ways. Would knowing this change how we decide, speak, think and act? It should. Our thoughts and words are scientifically proven to produce sound waves in the atmosphere and they always illicit a response. When we spew negativity, we get negativity. It is the same with positive thinking.

We have to DECIDE to have a good day. We have to DECIDE to be successful. We have to DECIDE to live and not just exist. Agree or not; YOU decide if you're going to be broke. Many of us are prone to excuses in times of lesson. However, you must realize that those are safety nets and cushioning to block the blow of reality. It is our fault. You may have been placed in a tested predicament and may have to exert much more effort. I've been there. While it's never felt fair, I can attribute a stronger feeling of accomplishment to the situation I worked through; the storm.

We are all more than capable. I've seen the molested raise loved children. I've seen the homeless gain (or regain) wealth. I've seen the abused, coach the many. I've seen the illiterate author write a best-seller. The only thing, the only person that could ever hold us back (especially amid all of the technology and tools at our fingertips) is the person we see, when we look at our reflections in the mirror.

I've been in a place where I felt defeated many times. My determination is what kept me going. Here are fifteen of my personal suggestions for a successful day:

1. Wake up early: You'll be surprised how much you get done those first hours, after you wake up.

2. Smile: Even if you're not feeling it; FORCE it! A smile produces endorphins that help to get your wheels spinning.

3. Exercise: More endorphins! Just 15-30 minutes will influence your diet and how you move throughout the day.

4. Meditate: Taking 10 minutes to focus on breathing and clearing negativity and mental blockages from your mind, will do wonders for your mental health

5. Affirmations: Remember when I said what you speak puts vibrations out into the universe? Saying things like "Money comes to me easily, frequently and in all kinds of ways" or "All of my friends are successful and add value to my life" daily will prove their worth. Find 10-20 great statements and repeat them daily.

6. Write your goals: They should be for the day, week, month, year and next five years. Adding dates will force your mind to work on reaching them by that date.

7. Read: Do more than the 43% of people, who only pick up one book after graduation. The average millionaire reads at least three books a month.

8. Plan: Write down your plans for the next day every night and review them before you sleep. Your brain will spend the night preparing for what needs to be done the next day.

9. Breathe: Take a few moments every few hours and breathe. We forget to take in the appropriate amount of breaths and our organs and muscles suffer from the lack of oxygen.

10. Be Social: There is a wealth of information and ideals that come from time spent around other people. Go out and soak up some knowledge or give it.

11. Travel: I've been known to leave the country for a day; for literally 24 hours. My son will also never have perfect attendance, because the best times to travel to many places are during the American school year. Travel is one of the best forms of education and it's the only thing that you can buy that makes you richer.

12. Dream: The one thing I like about the lottery, is that it gives those who don't dream a chance to dream! We've grown up having our dreams and fantasies put down at every turn and being brought back to reality. However, all millionaires, every

success story and every invention started as a dream. What are you passionate about?

13. Get Up: Learning to pick yourself up after going through shit, is a very important thing that no one ever teaches you. The fact that you got up, is MORE than half of the battle. The best comeback is the one from the valley.

14. Contentment: Your floor is always going to be someone else's ceiling. We must find contentment in all that we have, especially when we feel like we lack so much. If you can't find the blessing in your blessings, you won't be blessed with more.

15. Keep Going: The way we see ourselves, IS often the entire problem. We don't see who we are now but who we were in the past. We criticize ourselves so much, that we sell ourselves short. This hinders our true potential. As the saying goes, the successful person has failed more times than many have tried. I remember reading this

statement on a post: Where you're going is way more valuable than where you used to be!

We have discussed the imperative need to keep moving forward, to let go and to remember your why and reason for doing whatever it is you aim to do. We've also discussed remaining humble and the need to decide.

This is a snippet and a segue into a larger and more descriptive work, since my three main goals in life are to be the best example of all my best advice, to help others reach their potential and to gain wealth (in every way).

If you've gained at least one piece of value from this read, whether in relation to it or in something new to you, pay it forward. The goal is to help the many!

I do have one last suggestion: Give Thanks.

I am thankful to my son. He taught me empathy and adoration. I'm more emotional (annoyingly at times) because of him. Without my Amir, there would be no me.

I am thankful for my mother showing me the epitome of a strong woman. I've seen her rise through a lot. I also thank my siblings for forcing me to be the responsible person I am.

My grandparents are thanked for their amazing encouragement, because they've always made it clear how proud they are of me.

My dad has many of the qualities I want in my future husband. I have needed everything that I learned from him.

My friends (my closest friends) are the honest, loving, supportive ones we all need. They really do add value to my life!

I am thankful for all my business partners, because I've gained a great deal of knowledge from my time spent with them.

My mentors have been shining examples to me, who all somehow pushed me outside of my comfort zone.

I am very grateful to Stephanie, for allowing me the opportunity to participate in this work. It is certainly new territory for me, on the eve of my 32nd birthday and an amazing experience!

Thank you all!

Video Clip

Mother of 5 Stabbed to Death in a Parking Lot; The news report of Markesha's murder can be viewed at: https://youtu.be/2j2IbEmPeYs

WHEN YOU KNOW BETTER YOU DO BETTER

Stephanie Ford

Chapter 7

"Strength doesn't come from what you can do. It comes from overcoming the things you once thought you couldn't."

~ Nikki Rogers

I am not a quitter. Quitting just isn't an option. I don't even allow the letters to occupy my thoughts to then come up from my belly, seep out of my mouth, tiptoe across my lips and form into a word. Perseverance on the other hand, is constantly in my thoughts and actions. It takes a continuous effort to do or achieve something *despite* difficulties, failures, oppression and opposition.

My walk down perseverance street began when I was a teenager. What I didn't know then, was that I had begun a journey on a street that included stop signs, traffic lights and side streets that would lead to other streets, and other streets that would lead to forks in the road, or sometimes to roads that simply led to dead ends. Teenage parenting ain't easy. It does not smell like roses. Nonetheless, even if I could, I would not change my journey. I would still take a stroll down this street called *My Life*.

These streets were full of potholes and craters and at times were not paved at all. Nonetheless, I'd decided early on that quitting was not an option. I finished high school. My six-month old son was even in attendance at my graduation. It was a proud moment. Little did I know, the real learning was about to begin, since somebody had to feed this baby. The day he was born, I lost my freedom to do what other teenagers my age did after graduating. There would be no trunk party, college send-off, moving into a dorm or experiencing the life of a young adult who had just gotten her first taste of freedom. Freedom meant no parents breathing down your neck and the ability to act like a fool if you wanted to, because mommy and daddy were not looking. There would be no bonds formed with my college friends and no doing things that, when you look back, make you say to yourself, "What was I thinking?" I had to be at home. Still, all was not lost. Our journeys are supposed to be unique to us. For me, perseverance had grabbed hold, even before I fully understood what it meant. One week after graduation, I started my first real job -- a corporate job at a law firm.

My mother loved my sisters and me unconditionally and she loved our babies. When my son was born, he was fourth in the line of what would eventually become a tribe of ten grandkids -- nine boys and one girl. In my mother's eyes, those grandkids could do no wrong. She barely wanted them to stay out overnight with their daddies. She did not want them to stay with anybody. Despite my mother's love for our babies, she made it very clear that what she wasn't going to do, was babysit while we ran the streets. If you needed to go to work, have an interview, doctor's appointment or some other business to attend to, she had no problem. Otherwise, your baby went with you. She was giving us no space to make any "mistakes," by having more babies. She was a young grandmother and was still enjoying her life. My mother was living her best life, as a matter of fact. Her Saturday nights consisted of hanging out with her friends. Who were we to try to stop her, by asking her to babysit some adorable grandbabies?

Babies are a blessing, right? They are. Since I believe this, I had to take my blessing and learn my lesson, by bravely journeying down what was for me, an unpaved road. After working at my job for about six months, I realized that I was able to support myself and my son. I decided to move into my own apartment, when I was just 19. This took some courage. I did not move too far away from home. However, it was at least a twenty to thirty-minute ride by bus. What I didn't realize was the importance of budgeting and paying bills. I had just decided that because I could support us (my son and myself), that it was time to move. Besides, my mom's house was crowded with my sisters and those other cute babies. Of course, I had watched my mother growing up. I saw her pay bills, but was I really paying attention? I certainly wasn't asking any questions. When the rent is due, PECO and PGW are giving you the side eye, the day care or afterschool program needs to be paid and you and your son need to eat. However, if you can't pay them all, which one do you choose? When the child support payments come as infrequently, as the bus comes and you're running late for work, what do you do? This is the part of the road that is unpaved and full of potholes. Sometimes hitting a pothole and driving on an unpaved road shakes you up a bit. However, you learn to hold on and stay in control, until the road is smooth again. Strength of will and character is what helped me persevere through some extremely tough times as a young mother. I was not a quitter and I refused to become a quitter.

"You wanna fly, you got to give up the shit that weighs you down."

~Toni Morrison

Like so many young mothers, I had some baby daddy issues with my first son's father. He eventually got his mind right and started to consistently support my son financially, which was a help. As my son got older, I had more opportunities to hang out and do what 20 plus year-olds do. I dated here and there. I met a few . . . okay, I met a lot of immature guys my age. What did I expect? When I think about it now, I still meet immature guys my age. I guess they just need more time to catch up.

This new guy was just a tad bit different than the guys I had been meeting and dating. The guys in the club would buy you a few drinks, then think they were supposed to go home with you or you with them. Once they learned that I had my own place, they would immediately ask when they could come over, so that I could cook for them. Now, of course, I wasn't totally against having someone over and cooking them dinner but bruh, really? No in between and no talking on the phone for hours. There was no asking the usual getting to know you and your interest questions. There were no breakfast, lunch or dinner outings. There were also no movies, concerts or anything. We're just to immediately go from zero to 100? Where they do that at?

Despite my frequent encounters with too many immature men, somehow, this new guy caught my attention one day. I was just walking down the street, when I saw him. Right away, he came across as different. His first question was "When can I take you out?" That was different. First impressions are lasting impressions. My first impression of him is what made me say, "Yes, you can take me on a date and, of course, you can have my phone number." I was excited. He said that he would pick me up around 6:00 pm that evening. The plan was to see a movie and just hang out. I couldn't wait to tell my girlfriends all about it. To my surprise, he showed up on time. "Okay," I thought, "he earned a point there." Not only was he on time, but he drove up in a nice shiny car. Smiling inside, I said to myself, "I might just be impressed already."

The first time we met, he wore a baseball cap. Since this was a casual outing, he was dressed casually and he wore a baseball cap again. I settled into the car and put my seat belt on. I guess it was the law back then too. We shared some small talk and then it happened. He took off his hat. To say I was taken aback, surprised, shocked or that my mouth fell to the floor would be understatements. He said, "Do you like my haircut?" My first thought was that my friends were going to ask, "What are you doing with this old ass man?" He was just nine years older than me. I didn't have a problem with his age. However, his "haircut" with which he sported a nice close fade on the sides, revealed that he was definitely going bald on top. I wanted to scream "dude, it's time to let that hair go." Thankfully, he eventually said goodbye to the hair he was holding on to and just wore his head bald.

My phone rang and it was him. I was grinning hard. He asked if I wanted to take a ride with him. He said he would pick me up soon. It was a Saturday afternoon during the summer, so I freshened up very quickly and was ready when he pulled up. We were riding along and making small talk. I never asked where we were going, but I wanted to ask. We arrived at our destination. We pulled into a parking spot. I was looking around and there were just stores.

He grabbed my hand, as I got out of the car. We walked holding hands. He stopped in front of an ice cream store and said let's go in. We drove to Penn's Landing, after getting ice cream. We watched the water and talked some more. We talked a lot about the future. It was such a lovely feeling. Once home, I thought to myself, this was kind of nice. He was such a gentleman. However, eventually things changed.

"The car is gone! What happened to the car?" After looking out of the living room window and seeing that it was not there, I figured he must have driven it someplace while I was asleep. Then perhaps he parked it in a different parking space, but the only response I received when I asked what happened was, "I don't know." Was I in denial?

Much to my dismay, my new boyfriend wasn't so new anymore. The months were going by very fast. It had already been a year. We decided that he should move in. When my lease was up, we moved to a bigger apartment, since I'd already had my oldest son. He also had a daughter who would visit on the weekends. We found a nice place, but after dealing with unruly neighbors for about a year or so, we decided to move again. This time, we moved into a much nicer neighborhood. We were fortunate to have great neighbors, who also had kids. By now, I had a second son. We were doing okay. He even seemed to be staying on track. One evening he came in, went straight to the bedroom and then called my name. I walked in the room and he handed me a bag. In that bag, was a small box and in that box was . . . you guessed correctly – a ring. It was not just any ring. It was an engagement ring. It was my, "Issa getting married y'all moment," and I was so excited!

Rushing as usual, I pulled up to the daycare. I proceeded to get the kids out of the car and made sure to grab the hot wheels cars off the seat. Once inside, the boys never looked back. They found their usual buddies and playmates and settled down for a full day of fun. Outside, as I was leaving, I inquired as to whether my payment was received for the past two weeks. I'm still not sure what prompted me to ask. I also did not expect to receive the answer that I received. Was I in denial?"

Most engagements eventually lead to weddings. It took about five years, but we made it. The day was special. Lots of family and friends from both sides came to witness our union. Due to the size of both families and the astronomical cost it would have been for us to have our wedding at a venue, we decided instead to have it at a park. This way everyone could be invited. We didn't have a lot of bridesmaids and groomsmen. My mom was my Matron of Honor. His father was his Best Man.

I'd looked everywhere for the camera that I borrowed from my mother. I couldn't seem to find it. It should have been on the bookcase, where I left it when I last used it. I never did find it." Was I in denial?

Growing up in the crack era was sad and unfortunate for the African American community. The crack epidemic hit our communities especially hard. In his article entitled, *What the Crack Epidemic and Opioid Crisis Tell Us About Race in America,* CJ Quartlbaum explains:

> The crack epidemic is when crack cocaine flooded inner cities between the early 1980s and early 1990s. This highly addictive form of cocaine offered a faster and shorter high that ravaged neighborhoods. Crime rates surged, families broke apart, and countless lives were forever destroyed. Most black

people in the inner city during this time were touched in some way, even tangentially, by the horrors of this drug.

News outlets told horror stories of crack babies and their mothers, gang violence, fiends, and this drug that was devasting communities. The face of that drug was black. Its users were black. The problem was black. This reporting created a negative image in the minds of Americans. It went along with the false narratives that were already told of black people, since they were first brought here.

We called them pipers or crackheads. As far as I knew and saw, pipers were those otherwise regular folks, who got caught up in the epidemic. Unfortunately, this epidemic had taken over the black community. They were usually frail and thin with unkept clothing and hair. They were also known to have missing teeth. That crack sure did some damage to their teeth. Sometimes you would see someone clean and looking "normal," if there was such a thing for them. In my neighborhood the crackheads were most often people I had known for years.

Age wasn't a factor. Most were older than I was, but then there was a close family friend, who was my age. I felt bad for her. They were all caught up in the whirlwind of the crack epidemic. I never felt unsafe because of my familiarity with them. This was also around the time when I was hanging out at the club. My friends and I would meet up at the club. We lived in different neighborhoods, so after clubbing, we would go our separate ways when it was time to go home. After getting off the bus, I still had a few blocks to walk to get to my house. Well, at 2:00 am when I was returning from my night out with friends, the pipers were usually roaming the streets. I would see them, speak and keep it moving to my house. This is what addiction looked like to me.

It was early Saturday evening. I had just returned from being out all day running errands and entertaining kids. I hadn't spoken with him all day. I called to check in, but there was no answer. No big deal I thought, he'll be home later. Later came and went. My mind was consumed with all kinds of outrageous thoughts. Worry set in around 2:00 a.m. Then a level of pissivity (that's a word now) because how dare you not come home? I didn't want to alarm his parents, so I called my girlfriend and confided in her. First, I went through my anger stage of how pissed I was, neck rolling and talking about what I was going to say to him when he came home. That then turned to voicing my concerns of what if something happened, should I call the police? Should I call the hospitals? Around 7:00 a.m. the next morning, the doorbell rang. My heart dropped to my feet. After all, he had a key so who could it be? Upon opening the door, there he stood with one of his buddies. His friend said, "He's okay, Steph." For me, this was the first sign.

The apologies persisted for days. I was pissed, confused, unaware and consumed with working and taking care of my boys. I had never experienced such a thing. Before him, I lived alone. Although I was still unsure about this drug addiction or sickness as it is referred to, I *was* sure that I wasn't putting up with a man not coming home at night, unless he was dead. Otherwise, there was no excuse. We talked and he promised to get the help that he needed. What did help look like?

He had been acting strange. He was laid off from yet another job. I could not pinpoint exactly what was going on with him. He asked to use my car. He told me that he was running to the store and that he would be right back. Forty-five minutes later, he still wasn't back. I was so irritated! I called his phone repeatedly. He would not respond. The kids had been invited to a birthday party that day. Now, we were forty-five minutes late. After about two hours, my phone rang. It was him. He explained that the cops had taken my car, because his license was suspended. Yes, Live Stock, the policy of the Philadelphia Police Department (PPD) to enforce the impoundment provisions of the Pennsylvania Vehicle Code, was in full effect. He had parked in a bus zone. Who knew that his license was suspended? I had no idea. Anyway, there went $1,500 down the drain. We didn't even have the title to the car yet, because we had just purchased the car from an auction a week before this incident. The storage fees alone that would add up while we waited for the title, were so expensive that it was not even worth fighting to get the car back. Talk about a huge disappointment.

"No matter what happens, or how bad it seems today, life goes on, and it will be better tomorrow."
~Maya Angelou

Sometimes life just seems like one big struggle. That's if you don't change your thinking about struggle. Yes, the struggle *is* real! To make matters more complicated, the struggle often pertains to more than one area of your life. You may struggle in your relationships, your job, your housing situation, your children, or your family. We have all been through, will go through or are just coming out of some sort of struggle. How we handle what we learn from the struggles we face, is what is crucial.

As I think about things that I have struggled with, I try to answer this question. "What lesson am I supposed to take away from this situation?" If your car runs out of gas, your lesson is to make sure you have enough gas in your car for future trips. If you are in school and you fail a test or receive a low grade because you didn't study, the lesson you learn is to make sure you study more for the next test. Struggles contain vital lessons and when we look for these lessons and learn from them, we become better, stronger women every time.

I have never been a know it all type of woman. I don't know everything and know that I never will. However, what I know for sure, is that I will never let a struggle or a mistake that I made in life define me for the rest of my life. It takes courage, confidence and perseverance to overcome struggles and mistakes. You need courage to be able to stand and keep moving forward in the face of adversity. You simply have to **Get Cha Mind Right!** You have to take the loss, learn your lessons, change for the better and keep it moving. If you lie down and stop trying, life will run right over you.

Courage is strength or bravery in the face of pain. It took strength for me to share my truth in this chapter. It took a whole lot of strength to have a baby at seventeen years old, to graduate high school and be fortunate to find a decent job. It took strength for me to stay in a marriage for more than twenty years, when I knew that it was irreparable. It took strength for me to look each of my struggles in the eye and to keep moving and pushing forward.

Pushing forward means you must have courage, but it also means that you have to develop self-confidence. This combination of courage and self-confidence assure you that somehow you will be okay. It goes without saying, that all of this is much easier said than done. Self-confidence is something that you build up over time. For some people, it comes naturally. For others, like me, it takes some building -- years of building. I wasn't always confident in my abilities. I was not always comfortable with making hard decisions. My lack of self-confidence in making tough decisions, is one of the reasons I stayed in such an unhealthy relationship for so long. On the outside, I may have appeared confident, but the truth is that I was afraid. When fear backs you against a wall, you come out swinging and winning. For some people, confidence comes with maturity. That is what happened for me, or maybe there's just something special about turning forty and just not giving a damn anymore.

The struggle of living with a spouse addicted to drugs was REALLY REAL! Enduring my husband's addiction, while doing everything in my power to remain positive and raise my children, challenged me beyond what words can describe. I know that when you muster up the courage to face your struggles, it gives you the strength and confidence you need to overcome those struggles. Yes, facing your struggles gives you the confidence to overcome them. Most of all, courage and self-confidence give you the unique ability to persevere, over and over again.

Initially, I didn't even know what addiction to his drug of choice looked like. Therefore, I didn't notice the signs. As the non-addicted spouse, and as someone who has never been addicted to anything (okay, well maybe just an addiction to shoes), it was hard for me to even understand drug addiction as a disease. I still struggle with seeing addiction as a disease.

We always think that our situations are dire. However, in reality, they aren't. Although I was a teenage mom, I had support. There are some teenagers who get thrown out of the house, when their parents learn that they are pregnant. Luckily for me, that wasn't my reality. Still, those years of my life were extremely challenging. However, I was able to persevere, because I simply refused to let the situation define how my life would turn out. My marriage, like most marriages, had some ridiculously challenging times. Marriage is challenge -- period. Therefore, when you throw in drug addiction, being married becomes a ridiculous challenge on steroids! Nonetheless, I preserved through his addiction. Thankfully, so did he. Unfortunately, our marriage didn't.

As someone who is just not wired to quit, I'm also a firm believer that everything happens for a reason. I am proud of my story. Some of my life's best memories and accomplishments emerged from my fierce struggles with my marriage. Miraculously, all my experiences, both the good and the bad, have worked together for my good. Each of those experiences, make me the strong woman that I am right now. And so do all of yours.

Do not be ashamed of your story. Face your reality. Make the hard decisions. Be courageous and be confident in yourself.

Get Cha Mind Right, because YOU, my dear sister, are an exceptionally strong woman too!

About the Author

Stephanie T. Ford is a generous, dedicated and TIRELESS advocate for women's health and fitness. Her passion began with a focus on African American women, who are increasingly the demographic of individuals who most frequently die from diabetes and heart-related diseases. Ms. Ford is on a mission to reduce those statistics.

Ms. Ford has been unwavering in her commitment to the physical health and wellness of young girls and women in Philadelphia through her cycling and running volunteer and charitable initiatives. She is the *Founder of Pedal Posse Divas* (a women's cycling group that participates locally and abroad in bike rides to raise money for local and well-known national health charities), has hosted Women's Empowerment Conferences and Workshops focusing on women improving their physical and mental health and overall quality of life via her parent non-profit organization, "Get Cha Mind Right Inc.," where she has honored a Guinness World Record Holder in Bodybuilding and Fitness, Mrs. Ernestine Shephard; as well as implemented Morning Fitness Walks, and hosted Yoga Instructors who lead a group of women in fitness, relaxation and meditation sessions. Her annual conferences are extraordinary experiences that always sell out and that never fail please her guests.

Ms. Ford is a hardworking woman and because of that is a celebrated *Indego Ambassador with Independence Blue Cross' Bike Share Program* being recognized for surpassing all other Ambassadors in generating bike share memberships encouraging women to improve their health and fitness. She also started a lunchtime riding group of friends and office co-workers, with men and women riding together on Indego bikes during their lunch hour, which includes her teaching and insisting on adherence to helmet and bike safety guidelines.

The *Ignite Philly* organization invited Stephanie to be a featured speaker at a forum in a "Ted Talk" kind of program and recognized her accomplishments with a gift for her community and charitable work with Pedal Posse Divas. She was also a featured speaker at a Kayuh Bicycle's Event through "Gearing Up," whose program "uses biking as a tool to increase physical activity and lower stress . . . [to] help women adopt healthier lifestyles to combat histories of abuse, addiction, and incarceration."

Stephanie is the recipient of the 2017 *Philadelphia Magazine* Independence Blue Cross Health Hero award as a runner-up, the 2017 Legacy of Love Foundation Award for Non-Profits in Community Service in Philadelphia, and the 2016 William R. Klaus Community Award from Pepper Hamilton LLP, because of her commitment to her mission to improve the health and wellness of women and girls in the Philadelphia community.

Stephanie is not only a dreamer she is also a doer. If you know her, you know that she loves coffee and has always talked about opening a coffee shop. When an opportunity presented itself in 2018, Stephanie took advantage and is now the proud owner of *Coffee Cream & Dreams* which recently opened at 1500 Fairmount Avenue in the Fairmount section of Philadelphia. *Coffee Cream & Dreams* is a warm and welcoming café offering coffee, tea and a delicious variety of pastries.

Request Ms. Stephanie Ford to speak or train at your next event! Email your request to info@getchamindright.com or call 484-381-0471 today.

Made in the USA
Lexington, KY
22 November 2019

57560946R00116